Births, Marriages and Deaths on the Web

PART 2
The Midlands, Northern England and East Anglia

Stuart A. Raymond

Published by
The Federation of Family History Societies (Publications) Ltd.,
Units 15-16, Chesham Industrial Centre
Oram Street, Bury,
Lancashire BL9 6EN, UK

in association with
S.A. & M.J. Raymond
P.O. Box 35
Exeter, EX1 3YZ
Email: stuart@samjraymond.softnet.co.uk
Webpage: www.soft.net.uk/samjraymond.igb.htm

ISBNs:
Federation of Family History Societies: 1 86006 166 4
S.A. & M.J. Raymond 1 899668 34 9

First published 2002

Printed and bound by Alpha Print, Crawley Mill, Witney, Oxfordshire OX8 5TJ

Contents

Introduction

The records of births, marriages and deaths are vital resources for family historians. A rapidly increasing number of transcripts and indexes of these records are now available on the internet, and it is the purpose of this directory to identify the many web-pages where they, and various introductory information, can be found. Pages rather than sites are listed, as one site can include pages for numerous different places - Genuki being the obvious example.

This directory is primarily concerned with civil registration and parish registers, although associated records such as bishops transcripts, marriage licences, *etc.* are also mentioned. I have not, except in a few cases, listed the pages of particular registry offices, nor have I included pages devoted solely to particular surnames. Monumental inscriptions and war memorials are the subjects of separate directories.

Arrangement of this directory is by county. Each county is sub-divided into sections on civil registration, introductory pages on parish and non-parochial registers, county-wide indexes, collections of transcripts/indexes from a variety of places, pages relating to particular parishes, and a few other topics.

The titles of each web-page are given as they appear on the page; if no title is given on the page I have indicated this by enclosing my own wording in square brackets. If the title does not indicate the period covered I have tried to indicate this in a note. If the page is an index, rather than a transcript, this is also noted (although not entirely consistently). Where the web-page is taken from a book, a brief bibliographic note is included.

It is noticeable that, although a few facsimiles of published registers have been mounted on the web, there are virtually no facsimiles of the original documents. It is therefore, necessary to repeat the exhortation with which all good genealogical authors encourage their readers: check your sources! A transcript or index is only as accurate as the transcriber or indexer. Some are very good indeed; others are awful! If at all possible, you should always go back to the original record and check it.

This directory is equally liable to human error. If you are unable to find a URL listed here, you should enter either a part of the URL itself, or words from the title, into a search engine such as www.google.com. URL's change frequently, and no doubt a small proportion of those listed here will be out of date within a few months of publication. If you come across errors in this book, URL's that have changed, or new pages that ought to be listed, please let me know. It is hoped to produce new editions at frequent intervals, in order to help you keep track of the information currently available on the web.

This book has been typed by Cynthia Hanson, and seen through the press by Bob Boyd. My thanks go to them, and also to the officers of the Federation of Family History Society, whose support is vital to my work. My wife Marjorie, is also to be thanked for insisting that I should turn the computer off occasionally!

Stuart A. Raymond

Bedfordshire

Civil Registration
* Registration Districts in Bedfordshire
  www.fhsc.org.uk/genuki/reg/bdf.htm
  Between 1837 and 1930

* [St. Catherine's House Marriage Index, Jan-March, 1849. District 6.
  Bedfordshire/Berkshire/Hertfordshire]
  www.cs.ncl.ac.uk/genuki/StCathsTranscriptions/CATH4906.TXT

Parish and Non-Parochial Registers: Introductions and Lists
* About Bedfordshire Records
  www.rootsweb.com/~engbdf/records.html
  Mainly concerned with parish registers and associated records

* Genealogical Sources: Anglican Parish Registers
  www.bedfordshire.gov.uk/BedsCC/sdcountyrec.nsf/
  Enter and click on title. Lists registers at Bedfordshire and Luton
  archives and Records Office. Almost all pre-1813 registers have
  been published

* Genealogical Sources: Non-Anglican Registers
  www.bedfordshire.gov.uk/BedsCC/sdcountyrec.nsf/
  Enter and click on title. Lists registers at Bedfordshire and Luton
  Archives and Records Office

* Genealogical Sources: Non-Ecclesiastical Birth and Death Registers
  www.bedfordshire.gov.uk/BedsCC/sdcountyrec.nsf/
  Enter and click on title

* Bedfordshire: Quaker Family History Society
  www.rootsweb.com/engqfhs/Research/counties/beds.htm
  Lists registers *etc.*

Indexes
* Bedfordshire Parish Registers: Preparing a Master Index
  www.sigg.org.uk/arts/arts2601.htm
  Article from the Society of Indexers Genealogical Group

* Genealogical Sources: the Burial Indexes
  www.bedfordshire.gov.uk/BedsCC/sdcountyrec.nsf/
  Enter and click on title. Brief list

* Bedfordshire, England: Parish and Probate Records
  www.beliefnet.ancestry.com/search/rectype/inddbs/5843.htm
  Database based on published registers, *etc.*

* IGI Batch Numbers for Bedford, England
  freepages.genealogy.rootsweb.com/~hughwallis/IGIBatchNumbers/
  CountyBedford.htm

* Free Reg: Bedfordshire
  freereg.rootsweb.com/parishes/bdf/index.htm
  Details of the registers currently included in a project to index births,
  deaths and marriages.

Publications
* Bedfordshire Parish Register Series
  www.bfhs.org.uk
  Click on 'Publication List' and 'Bedfordshire Parish Register Series'.
  Bedfordshire is unique in having all its pre-1812 registers available in
  printed form or on fiche. The fiche are listed here.

Great Barford
* Great Barford Parish Records
  www.sgibbs1.freeserve.co.uk/gtbarford/
  Baptisms 1831-1892; marriages 1813-1904; burials 1841-1900.

Toddington
* Toddington Family History Resource Page
  www.toddington.net/hist.htm
  Baptisms, marriages and burials from the 16th c.

Turvey
* Turvey's Non-conformists
  www.turvey.homestead.com/nonconform.html
  Includes list of burials

Cambridgeshire

Civil Registration
- Registration Districts in Cambridgeshire
  www.fhsc.org.uk/genuki/reg/cam.htm

- Cambridgeshire County Council Registration of Births Index
  atoz1.camcnty.gov.uk/rbdm/ridbirths.nsf/search?OpenForm

- Cambridgeshire County Council Registration of Marriages Index
  atoz1.camcnty.gov.uk/rbdm/ridmars.nsf/search?OpenForm

- Cambridgeshire County Council Registration of Deaths Index
  atoz1.camcnty.gov.uk/riddeaths.nsf/search?OpenForm

- [St. Catherine's House Marriage Index. Jan-March, 1849. District 14. Cambridgeshire/Lincolnshire]
  www.cs.ncl.ac.uk/genuki/StCathsTranscriptions/CATH4914.TXT

Parish & Non-Parochial Registers: Introduction & Lists
- Original Parish Registers at the County Record Office, Cambridge
  www.genuki.org.uk/big/eng/CAM/OriginalParishRegisters.html
  List

- Microfilm Holdings of Parish Registers & Bishops Transcripts at the County Record Office, Cambridge
  www.genuki.org.uk/big/eng/CAM/
  CambridgeshireRecordOfficeMicrofilmHoldings.html
  List

- Cambridgeshire
  www.sog.org.uk/prc/caambridgeshire.html
  Parish registers, printed, typescript, etc., in the library of the Society of Genealogists

- Cambridgeshire Methodism
  www.rootsweb.com/~engcam/method.htm
  Lists Methodist registers

- Quaker Family History Society: Cambridgeshire
  www.rootsweb.com/~engqfhs/Research/counties/cambs.htm
  Lists Quaker registers, etc.

- Cambridgeshire Society of Friends (Quakers)
  www.rootsweb.com/~engcam/quakers.htm
  Includes notes on registers

Indexes
- Cambridgeshire Baptism Index 1801-37
  www.cfhs.org.uk/BaptismIndex/
  On-line database

- Cambridgeshire Family History Society: Boyds Marriage Index 1538-1600
  www.cfhs.org.uk/BoydsMarriageIndex/index.html
  Searchable database for Cambridgeshire

- Cambridgeshire Burial Index (1801-1837)
  www.cfhs.org.uk/BurialIndex/
  On-line database

- Parishes covered by Boyds Marriage Index: Cambridgeshire
  www.englishorigins.com/bmi-parishstats.asp?county=Cambridgeshire

- Cambridgeshire, England: Parish and Probate Records
  www.ancestry.com/search/locality/main.htm?uk
  Click on 'England'; then on 'Cambridgeshire'. Index to published registers, etc.

- IGI Batch Numbers: Cambridgeshire Batch Numbers
  freepages.genealogy.rootsweb.com/~tyeroots/cambridge.html

- IGI Batch Numbers for Cambridge, England
  freepages.genealogy.rootsweb.com/~hughwallis/IGIBatchNumbers/
  CountyCambridge.htm

Strays
- Cambridgeshire Strays with Marriages and Banns
  www.rootsweb.com/~engcam/Strays/StraysMarriagesBanns.html

Christchurch
- Christchurch Parish Registers: Transcript Index
freepages.genealogy.rootsweb.com/~cawthorn/transcripts/
                                                   trans-index.html

  Brief extracts, 19-20th c.

Ely
- Cholera in the 19th century
www.rootsweb.com/~engcam/cholera.htm
Includes list of Ely victims 1832

Leverington
- Leverington Marriage Index 1626-1675
www.cfhs.org.uk/LeveringtonMarriages1626-1675/

Orwell
- The Marriage Register of the Parish of Orwell 1653 to 1837
www.orwell.uk.com/orwell%20marriage%20register.htm

Wimpole
- The Wimpole Registers 1560-1863
www.wimpole.uk.com/wimpole%20registers.htm

Wisbech
- Index of Selected Marriages from 1560-1827 for Wisbech St. Peter, CAM., England
genea-logos.bizhosting.com/wisbech/indexes/wis__p.htm

Cheshire

Civil Registration
- Registration Districts in Cheshire
www.fhsc.org.uk/genuki/reg/chs.htm
Between 1837 and 1930

- Cheshire Registration Service
www.cheshire.gov.uk/register/home.htm

- Cheshire BMD: Births, Marriages and Deaths on the Internet
cheshirebmd.org.uk
Index in progress, covering civil registration records 1837 - 1950. Important

- [St. Catherine's House Marriage Index, Jan-March, 1849. District 19. Cheshire/Derbyshire]
www.cs.ncl.ac.uk/genuki/StCathsTranscriptions/CATH4919.TXT

- [St. Catherine's House Marriage Index, Jan-March, 1849. District 18. Cheshire/Shropshire]
www.cs.ncl.ac.uk/genuki/StCathsTranscriptions/CATH4918.TXT

Parish and Non-Parochial Registers: Introductions & Lists
- Cheshire Methodist Registers in the Public Record Office, London, England.
www.geocities.com/Heartland/Plains/8555/prometh.html

- Cheshire
www.sog.org.uk/prc/chs.html
Parish registers, printed, typescript, *etc.,* in the library of the Society of Genealogists

- Quaker Family History Society: Cheshire
www.rootsweb.com/engqfhs/Research/counties/cheshire.htm
Notes on Quaker records

Indexes
- IGI Batch Numbers: Cheshire Batch Numbers
freepages.genealogy.rootsweb.com/~tyeroots/cheshire.html

- IGI Batch Numbers for Cheshire, England
  freepages.genealogy.rootsweb.com/~hughwallis/IGIBatchNumbers/
  CountyCheshire.htm

Transcript Collections on the Web
- Cheshire Parish Register Project
  www.mimas.ac.uk/~mfscprdb/
  Project to transcribe all Cheshire registers. Those already available and fully described (as at April 2002) are separately listed below. Many other parishes are well-advanced. Currently, only access by form-filling is available to casual users. Important

Publications
- Family History Society of Cheshire. Microfiche Publications
  www.fhsc.org.uk/fich.htm
  Mainly monumental inscriptions and parish registers

- Cheshire Burials
  www.genuki.org.uk/big/eng/CHS/NorthChesFHS/Cheshire__Burials.htm
  List of parish register burial entries on fiche from North Cheshire Family History Society.

- South Cheshire Family History Society Publications
  www.scfhs.org.uk/pubs.html
  Includes parish registers and monumental inscriptions.

Bromborough
- Parish Notes: Bromborough 1600-1870
  www.mimas.ac.uk/~mfscprdb
  Click on 'Progress' and placename for discussion of the transcription and on 'Database' to search specific surnames.

Burton
- Parish Notes: Burton 1538-1870
  www.mimas.ac.uk/~mfscprdb
  Click on 'Progress' and placename for discussion of the transcription, and on 'Database' to search specific surnames.

Chester
- Methodist Death Notices from St. John Circuit, Chester, 1803-1900
  www.geocities.com/Heartland/Plains/8555/obit.html

Heswall
- Parish Notes: Heswall 1539 - 1871
  www.mimas.ac.uk/~mfscprdb
  Click on 'Progress' and placename for discussion of the transcription, and on 'Database' to search specific surnames.

Kelsall
- Parish Registers, Kelsall, Cheshire
  www.the-dicksons.org/Kelsall/kelsall/parish.htm
  Includes St. Philips marriage register 1869-99, and extracts from Kelsall Methodist church burial register 1916-88.

Neston
- Parish Notes: Neston 1559-1871
  www.mimas.ac.uk/~mfscprdb
  Click on 'Progress' and placename for discussion of the transcription, and on 'Database' to search specific surnames.

West Kirby
- Parish Notes: West Kirby 1561-1871
  www.mimas.ac.uk/~mfscprdb
  Click on 'Progress' and placename for discussion of the transcription, and on 'Database' to search specific surnames.

Whitegate
- Parish Notes: Whitegate 1565-1971
  www.mimas.ac.uk/~mfscprdb
  Click on 'Progress' and placename for discussion of the transcription, and on 'Database' to search specific surnames.

Cumberland

Civil Registration
- Civil Registration
  www.genuki.org.uk/big/eng/CUL/registr.html
  In Cumbria

- Registration Districts in Cumberland
  www.fhsc.org.uk/genuki/reg/cul.htm
  Between 1837 and 1930

- Cumbria Genealogy: the St. Catherine's Marriage Index for March quarter, 1849
  members.netscapeonline.co.uk/rolygrigg/ StCatsMarchQr1849Marriages.html
  For Cumberland and Westmorland

- Cumbrian Genealogy: St. Catherines Marriages 1856/Q1. Volume 10a, 10b
  members.netscapeonline.co.uk/rolygrigg/StCaths1856Qr1Marriages.html
  For Cumberland

Parish and Non-Parochial Registers: Introductory and Lists
- Cumberland
  www.sog.org.uk/prc/cumberland.html
  Parish registers, printed, typescript, *etc.,* in the library of the Society of Genealogists

- Quaker Family History Society: Cumberland
  www.rootsweb.com/~engqfhs/Research/counties/cumberlnd.htm
  Notes on Quaker records (including the Isle of Man)

Indexes
- Cumbrian Genealogy: Parish Registers Index
  www.btinternet.com/~grigg/ParRegsIndex.htm

- Parishes covered by Boyd's Marriage Index: Cumberland
  www.englishorigins.com/bmi-parishstats.asp?county=Cumberland

- IGI Batch Numbers: Cumberland Batch Numbers
  freepages.genealogy.rootsweb.com/~tyeroots/cumb.html

- IGI Batch Numbers for Cumberland, England
  freepages.genealogy.rootsweb.com/~hughwallis/IGIBatchNumbers/ CountyCumberland.htm

Transcript Collections on the Web
- Cumbrian Genealogy: Parish Registers
  johnwatters.members.beeb.net
  Many pages of transcripts for Cumberland and Westmorland, separately listed below

Publications
See also Durham
- C.W.A.A.S. Publications
  www.cwaas.org.uk/publications.htm
  Includes a few parish registers

Alston
- Cumbrian Genealogy: Alston Marriages 1701-1783
  johnwatters.members.beeb.net/AlstonAtoE.htm
  Index continued on 3 further pages

- Marriages from the Alston registers (1701-1783)
  www.genuki.org.uk/big/eng/CUL/Alston/MALS1701.html

- Marriages from the Alston Registers (1784-1812)
  www.genuki.org.uk/big/eng/CUL/Alston/MALS1784.html

- Marriages from the Alston Registers (1813-1837)
  www.genuki.org.uk/big/eng/CUL/Alston/MALS1813.html

Bassenthwaite
- The Oldest Parish Registers of Bassenthwaite
  www.btinternet.com/~grigg/Bassenthwaite.html
  Originally published in the *Transactions of the Cumberland & Westmorland Antiquarian & Archaeological Society* 1965. Extracts for selected names only.

Garrigill
- Baptisms from the Garrigill registers 1813-1837
  www.genuki.org.uk/big/eng/CUL/Garrigill/XGAR.html

- Marriages from the Garrigill Registers 1730-1837
  www.genuki.org.uk/big/eng/CUL/Garrigill/MGAR.html

- Cumbrian Genealogy: Garrigill Marriages, 1730-1837, and Baptisms 1813-1837
  johnwatters.members.beeb.net/garigill.htm

Great Orton

- Cumbrian Genealogy: Parish Register of St. Giles, Gt. Orton 1568-1812
  johnwatters.members.beeb.net/OrtonABC855.htm
  Index continued on 4 further pages.

Lamplugh

- Cumbrian Genealogy: Lamplugh Parish Register 1581-1812
  johnwatters.members.beeb.net/LamplughAB910.htm
  Index continued on 6 further pages.

Matterdale

- Matterdale and Watermillock
  edenlinks.rootsweb.com/1gp/RECORDS/MATTEX.HTM
  Includes Matterdale register 1634-57, marriages 1634-1910, Wesleyan Methodist Chapel of Matterdale and Watermillock baptisms register, *etc.*

Newton Reigny

- Cumbrian Genealogy: Newton Reigny Parish Register 1571-1812
  johnwatters.members.beeb.net/NewtonReignyAtoG.htm
  Continued on 3 further pages

Penrith

- Cumbrian Genealogy: The Registers of St. Andrew's Parish Church, Penrith
  johnwatters.members.beeb.net/Penrith1AtoB.html
  Index, 1556-1604. Continued on 6 further pages.

- Cumbrian Genealogy: The Registers of St. Andrew's Parish Church, Penrith
  johnwatters.members.beeb.net/Penrith2AtoB.html
  Index, 1605-1660. Continued on 7 further pages.

Skelton

- Cumbrian Genealogy: Skelton Parish Register 1680-1812
  johnwatters.members.beeb.net/SkeltonAB.htm
  Continued on 9 further pages

Watermillock
See Matterdale

Wigton

- Cumbrian Genealogy: The Parish Registers of Wigton, Cumberland: Baptisms 1604-1727
  johnwatters.members.beeb.net/wig1bap1.html
  Continued on 2 further pages

- Cumbrian Genealogy: Registers of Wigton: Baptisms 1729-1797
  johnwatters.members.beeb.net/wig2bap1.html
  Index. Continued on 3 further pages.

- Cumbrian Genealogy: The Parish Registers of Wigton, Cumberland: Marriages 1604-1727
  johnwatters.beeb.net/wig1mar1.html
  Index. Continued on 2 further pages.

- Cumbrian Genealogy: Registers of Wigton: Marriages 1728-81
  johnwatters.beeb.net/wig2Marr1.html
  Index. Continued on 3 further pages

- Cumbrian Genealogy: The Registers of Wigton: Burials 1604-1727
  johnwatters.beeb.net/wig1bur1.html
  Continued on 3 further pages

- Cumbrian Genealogy: Registers of Wigton: Burials 1728-1779
  johnwatters.beeb.net/wig2bur1.html
  Continued on 2 further pages

Derbyshire

Civil Registration
- Registration Districts in Derbyshire
  www.fhsc.org.uk/genuki/reg/dby.htm
  Between 1837 and 1930

- Derbyshire District Registrars
  www.genealogy-links.co.uk/html/dby.dist.reg.html
  Addresses

Parish & Non-Conformist Registers: Introductory Pages & Lists
- Derbyshire
  www.sog.org.uk/prc/derbyshire.html
  Parish registers, printed, typescript, *etc.,* in the library of the Society of Genealogists

- Quaker Family History Society: Derbyshire
  www.rootsweb.com/~engqfhs/Research/counties/derby.htm
  Notes on Quaker records

Indexes
- Derbyshire, England: Parish and Probate Records
  www.ancestry.com/search/rectype/inddbs/5863.htm
  Index of published registers

- Free Reg: Derbyshire
  freereg.rootsweb.com/parishes/dby/index.htm
  Details of the registers currently included in a project to index births, marriages and deaths.

- IGI Batch Numbers: Derbyshire Batch Numbers
  freepages.genealogy.rootsweb.com/~tyeroots/derby.html

- IGI Batch Numbers for Derby, England
  freepages.genealogy.rootsweb.com/~hughwallis/IGIBatchNumbers/
  CountyDerby__(A-M).htm
  Coninued at **/CountyDerby__(N-Z).htm**

Transcript Collections on the Web
- Derbyshire: Records of Marriages in individual parishes
  homepages.ntlworld.com/sherwoodoutlaw/derbyshiremarriageindex.htm
  Pages for individual parishes separately listed below

- Repton & Gresley Hundred, South Derbyshire: Parish Register Transcripts
  freepages.genealogy.rootsweb.com/~brett/parregs.htm

Alvaston
- Alvaston 1614-1812: Brides
  homepage.ntlworld.com/sherwoodoutlaw/alvastonbride.htm
  Index

- Alvaston 1614-1812: Grooms
  homepage.ntlworld.com/sherwoodoutlaw/alvastongroom.htm
  Index

Ashbourne
- Matters of life and death: history in baptisms, marriages and burials as recorded in the parish registers of St. Oswald's Parish Church, Ashbourne, Derbyshire, England, 1539 to 1945
  www.ashbourne-town.com/frame1.html
  Selected extracts only

Ashover
- Baptisms, Marriages and Burials at All Saints Church, Ashover
  www.genuki.org.uk/big/eng/DBY/Ashover/CDAllSaints.html
  Details of a CD

- Ashover: a guide for genealogists
  dspace.dial.pipex.com/goth/
  Includes baptisms, marriages and burials, 17-20th c.

- Weddings at All Saints Church, from 1642-1724
  familytreemaker.genealogy.com/users/m/i/l/John-Mills/FILE/
  0003page.html?Welcome=1016031173

  At Ashover

- Quaker Burials at Buntingfield/Peasonhurst
  dspace.dial.pipex.com/goth/quakbur.htm
  In Ashover parish

- Moor Road Weslyan Methodist Church Baptisms
  dspace.dialpipex.com/goth/moorrd1.htm
  In Ashover

- Moor Road Wesleyan Methodist Church Marriages
  dspace.dial.pipex.com/goth/moorroadmar.htm
  In Ashover

- Ashover United Methodist Free Church (Butts Chapel) Baptisms
  dspace.dial.pipex.com/goth.butts1.htm

Baslow
- Some Notes from Baslow Parish Registers 1688-1737, 1738-51, 1752-1804
  www.genuki.org.uk/big/eng/DBY/Baslow/PRNotes.html
  Mainly notes; few baptisms, marriages and deaths.

Brampton
- Parish of Brampton
  homepages.rootsweb.com/~spire/brampton/default.htm
  Includes births and baptisms, 1832-51, burials 1832-1974

- British Vital Records Index
  homepages.rootsweb.com/%7Espire/chesterfield/buri.htm
  Index to births/baptisms and marriages for Brampton

Brassington
- Brassington Residents Database
  www.brassington.org/database.htm
  Index to parish registers and various other sources

Brimington
- Brimington
  www.skimber.demon.co.uk/brim/brim.htm
  Includes births/baptisms and burials/deaths from various sources, 20th c.

Buntingfield
  See Ashover

Chapel en le Frith
- St. Thomas a Beckett Parish Registers
  freepages.genealogy.rootsweb.com/~dusk/chapel-e-l-f__pr.htm
  Baptisms (selected) 1621-1874; marriages (selected) 1622-1862, and burials (selected) 1622-1907.

Charlesworth
- St. Mary's Independent Chapel, Charlesworth
  freepages.genealogy.rootsweb.com/charlesworth__ind__chapel.htm
  Selected baptisms, 1789-1833, and burials, 1852-1904

Chellaston
- Chellaston 1570-1812: Brides
  homepage.ntlworld.com/sherwoodoutlaw/chellastonbride.htm
  Index

- Chellaston 1570-1812: Grooms
  homepage.ntlworld.com/sherwoodoutlaw/chellastongroom.htm
  Index

Chesterfield
- The Dissenters Register
  homepages.rootsweb.com/~spire/chesterfield/dissenters.htm
  Originally published in *The history of Chesterfield*, 1890. Covers 1710-32.

Chinley
- Chinley Independent Chapel Baptisms
  freepages.genealogy.rootsweb.com/~dusk/ chinly__ind__chapel__baptisms.html

- Chinley Independent Chapel Marriages
  freepages.genealogy.rootsweb.com/~dusk/ chinely__ind__chapel__marriages.html

- Chinley Independent Chapel Burials
  freepages.genealogy.rootsweb.com/~dusk/ chinley__ind__chapel__burials.html
  Selected entries only, 1703 to 1805 and 1838-1908; Complete transcript 1806-1837

Church Gresley
- Parish & Non-Conformist Registers: Church Gresley
  freepages.genealogy.rootsweb.com/~brett/gresley/gresley.htm#Parish
  List registers, transcripts, films, *etc.*

- Church Gresley, St. Mary & St. George's Baptisms 1841-1845
  freepages.genealogy.rootsweb.com/~brett/parregs/cgbap__a.htm
  Continued to 1860, with separate surname index, on 5 further pages.

- Church Gresley, St. Mary & St. George's: Marriages 1783-1800
  freepages.genealogy.rootsweb.com/~brett/parregs/cgmar__00.htm
  Continued to 1883, with separate index, on 20 further pages.

- Church Gresley, St. Mary & St. Georges: Burials 1695-1720
  freepages.genealogy.rootsweb.com/~brett/parregs/cgbur__1720.htm
  Continued to 1812, with surname index, on 6 further pages.

Crich

- Crich Parish Registers: Marriage, Baptism, Burial
  freepages.genealogy.rootsweb.com/~dlhdby/parish.htm
  1813-25

Darley Dale

- Baptisms, Marriages and Burials at St. Helen's Church, Darley Dale
  www.genuki.org.uk/big/eng/DBY/DarleyDale/CDStHelen.html
  Details of CD

Derby

- Derby, St. Peter's 1558-1812. Brides
  homepage.ntlworld.com/sherwoodoutlaw/
  derbystpetersbridefrontpage.htm
  Index

- Derby, St. Peters 1558-1812: grooms
  homepage.ntlworld.com/sherwoodoutlaw/
  derbystpetersgroomfrontpagehtm.htm
  Index

Dethick

- Parish Registers
  freepages.genealogy.rootsweb.com/~dlhdby/parishreg.htm
  Dethick baptisms 1774-1781 and 1813-1820.

Donisthorpe

- Parish Registers
  freepages.genealogy.rootsweb.com/~brett/donisthorpe/
  donisthorpe.htm#Parish
  Of Donisthorpe and Oakthorpe. List of parish registers, transcripts, films, *etc.*

Duffield

- Parish Registers and Churchwardens Books
  www.derwent99.freeserve.co.uk/duffield/11rgstr.htm
  General discussion of the Duffield register. Not a transcript.

Eyam

- Extracts of Eyam Parish Records
  www.genuki.org.uk/big/eng/DBY/Eyam/Records.html
  Names from a variety of sources, including the parish register, bishops transcripts, monumental inscriptions, *etc.*

- The Plague book of Eyam
  www.geocities.com/Heartland/Acres/8040/plague.html
  Includes list of plague victims 1666.

Hartshorne

- Hartshorne.org.uk
  www.hartshorne.org.uk
  Click on 'Archives', and choose from 'Births', 'Marriages', 'Deaths', 'Parish registers'

- Parish & Non-Conformist Registers: Hartshorne
  freepages.genealogy.rootsweb.com/~brett/hartshorne/
  hartshornehtml#Parish
  Lists registers, transcripts, films, etc.

Hayfield

- St. Matthews Church, Hayfield
  freepages.genealogy.rootsweb.com/~dusk/hayfield__pr.html
  Selected baptisms 1754-1873, and burials 1640-1918

Heage

- Heage Parish Church Baptisms Register
  www.spendlovej.freeserve.co.uk/ancestral/heage__baptisms.html
  Covers 1819-38. Alphabetical index

- Heage Parish Church Burials 1847 to 1864
  www.spendlovej/ancestral/heage__bur2/heage__burials1.html
  Alphabetical index

- Heage Parish Church Burials
  www.spendlovej.freeserve.co.uk/ancestral/
  heage__bur/heage__burials.html
  Alphabetical index for 1864-78

Heanor

- St. Lawrence Church, Heanor Baptism Records for 1816 to 1837
  **www.spendlovej.freeserve.co.uk/
  ancestral/hsl__1816-1837/saint__lawrence1.html**

- St. Lawrence Church, Heanor Baptism Records for 1837 to 1894
  **www.spendlovej.freeserve.co.uk/
  ancestral/hsl__1837-1894/saint__lawrence.html**

Hope

- Notes from a Peakland Parish: an account of the Church and Parish of Hope in the County of Derby, chapter V: Some Notes on the Parish Register
  www.genuki.org.uk/big/eng/DBY/Hope/Notes/ChapterV.html
  General discussion with some extracts

Kirk Langley

- Kirk Langley 1654-1812: Brides
  homepage.ntlworld.com/sherwoodoutlaw/kirklangleybride.htm
  Index

- Kirk Langley 1654-1812: grooms
  homepage.ntlworld.com/sherwoodoutlaw/kirklangleygroom.htm
  Index

Matlock

- Matlock Surnames from Baptism, Marriage and Burial entries in the parish registers for Matlock, Derbyshire, England, 1637-1856
  www.wirksworth.org.uk/MK-X-01.htm

- Baptisms, Marriages and Burials at St. Giles Church, Matlock
  www.genuki.org.uk/big/eng/DBY/Matlock/CDStGiles.html
  Details of a CD

- Matlock Marriages 1637-1837: Index of Brides and Grooms
  www.andrewspages.dial.pipex.com/matlock/marriage.htm
  Partially based on the Phillimore transcript

Monyash

- Quaker Marriages - Monyash
  dspace.dial.pipex.com/goth/quakmar.htm

Newbold

- Newbold Births and Baptism
  freepages.genealogy.rootsweb.com/~spire/newbold/births.htm

- Burials & Deaths - Newbold
  freepages.genealogy.rootsweb.com/~spire/newbold/newboldburials.htm

Newhall

- Newhall Baptisms 1833
  freepages.genealogy.rootsweb.com/~brett/newbap33.htm
  Continued to 1882 on annual pages, with separate surname index

- Newhall Marriages 1845-1850
  freepages.genealogy.rootsweb.com/~brett/newmar50.htm
  Continued to 1877, with separate surname index, on 8 further pages

- Newhall Burials 1833
  freepages.genealogy.rootsweb.com/~brett/newbur33.htm
  Continued to 1865 on annual pages, with separate surname index on 6 pages

Newton Solney

- Newton Solney Baptisms 1663-1675
  freepages.genealogy.rootsweb.com/~brett/nsbap1663__1675.htm
  Continued to 1761, with separate surname index, on 8 further pages

- Newton Solney Marriages 1663-1754
  freepages.genealogy.rootsweb.com/~brett/nsmar1663-1754.htm
  Continued to 1836, with surname index, on 5 further pages

- Newton Solney Burials 1663-1675
  freepages.genealogy.rootsweb.com/~brett/nsbur1663__1675.htm
  Continued to 1812, with surname index, on 10 further pages

Normanton

- Normanton by Derby 1769-1810: Brides
  homepage.ntlworld.com/sherwoodoutlaw/normantonbride.htm
  Index

- Normanton by Derby 1769-1810: Grooms
  homepage.ntlworld.com/sherwoodoutlaw/normantongroom.htm
  Index

North Wingfield

- Baptisms, Marriages and Burials at St. Lawrence's Church, North Wingfield
  www.genuki.org.uk/big/eng/DBY/Northwingfield/CDStLawrence.html
  Details of a CD, including some entries for Clay Cross and Pilsley

Oakthorpe

See Donisthorpe

Osmaston

- Osmaston by Derby 1743-1812: Brides
  homepage.ntlworld.com/sherwoodoutlaw/osmastonbride.htm
  Index

- Osmaston by Derby 1743-1812: Grooms
  homepage.ntlword.com/sherwoodoutlaw/osmastongroom.htm
  Index

Peak Forest

- The Marriage Registers of Peak Forest Chapel, Derbyshire
  www.genuki.org.uk/big/eng/DBY/PeakForest/about.html
  From the edition edited by G. W. Marshall and published in 1901

- Foreign Marriages in Peak Forest Chapel 1727-1754
  www.genuki.org.uk/big/eng/DBY/PeakForest/pftext.html

- Other Marriages in Peak Forest Chapel 1729-March 1815
  www.genuki.org.uk/big/eng/DBY/PeakForest/pftext2.html

Peasonhurst

See Ashover

Pilsley

See North Wingfield

Pinxton

- Pinxton 1561-1812: Brides
  homepage.ntlworld.com/sherwoodoutlaw/pinxtonbrides.htm
  Index

- Pinxton 1561-1821: Grooms
  homepage.ntlworld.com/sherwoodoutlaw/pinxtongrooms.htm
  Index

Stapenhill

- Stapenhill Baptisms 1770-1779
  freepages.genealogy.rootsweb.com/~brett/stabap01.htm
  Continued to 1800, with surname index, on 5 further pages

Stoney Middleton

- Extracts of Stoney Middleton Parish Records
  www.genuki.org.uk/big/eng/DBY/StoneyMiddleton/Records.html

Tansley

- Holy Trinity Church: indexes to baptism, marriage and burial registers 1840-1899
  freespace.virgin.net/denys.gaskell/tansley.html
  At Tansley

Tideswell

- The Feudal History of the County of Derby, volume 5, chapter 16: Parish Registers
  www.genuki.org.uk/big/eng/DBY/Yeatman/Volume5/Chapter16.html
  For Tideswell, 1635-1800

Whittington

- Burials & Deaths
  homepages.rootsweb.com/~spire/whittington/death.htm
  At Whittington, 19th c., from various sources

Willington

- Willington 1698-1812: Brides
  homepage.ntlworld.com/sherwoodoutlaw/willingtonbride.htm
  Index

- Willington 1698-1812: Grooms
  homepage.ntlworld.com/sherwoodoutlaw/willingtongroom.htm
  Index

Wirksworth

- Wirksworth Parish Records 1600-1900
  www.wirksworth.org.uk
  Includes parish registers, 1608-1899, memorial inscriptions, 1555-1991, *etc.*

Woodville

- Woodville St. Stephens Baptisms 1847-1853
  freepages.genealogy.rootsweb.com/~brett/parregs/woodbap__a.htm
  Continued to 1872, with separate surname index, on 4 further pages.
  Also available (with continuation to 1908) at
  /~brett/woodville/wood__bap50.htm

- Woodville St. Stephens Marriages 1848-1862
  freepages.genealogy.rootsweb.com/~brett/parregs/woodmar__a.htm
  Continued to 1881, with separate surname index, on 3 further pages.
  Also available (with continuation to 1900) at:
  /~brett/woodville/wood__marr60.htm

- Woodville St. Stephens Burials 1847-1862
  freepages.genealogy.rootsweb.com/~brett/parregs/woodbur__a.htm
  Continued to 1882, with separate index, on 3 further pages. Also
  available (with continuation to 1860) at:
  /~brett/woodville/wood__bur60.htm

Durham

Civil Registration
- Registration Districts in Durham
  www.fhsc.org.uk/genuki/reg/dur.htm
  Between 1837 and 1930

- Durham County Record Office User Guide 1: A Brief Guide to Civil
  Registration
  www.durham.gov.uk/durhamcc/usp.nsf/lookup/pdfhandlists/$file/
  userguide01.pdf

- [St.Catherine's House Marriage Index, Jan-March, 1849. District 24.
  County Durham/Northumberland]
  www.cs.ncl.ac.uk/genuki/StCathsTranscriptions/CATH4924.TXT

Parish & Non-Parochial Registers: Introductory Pages & Lists
- Durham County Record Office. Handlist 2. Parish Registers
  www.durham.gov.uk/durhamcc/usp.nsf/lookup/pdfhandlists/$file/
  handlists02.pdf

- Church of England Parishes in Co. Durham
  www.durham.gov.uk/recordoffice/dro.nsf/web/parishes
  List of parishes with details of parish registers available at Durham
  Record Office

- Durham County Record Office Handlist 3: Modern Transcripts and
  Indexes (Church of England)
  www.durham.gov.uk/durhamcc/usp.nsf/lookup/pdfhandlists/$file/
  handlist03.pdf

- Durham County Record Office User Guide 7: Guide to Census and
  Parish Register Microfilms
  www.durham.gov.uk/durhamcc/usp.nsf/lookup/pdfhandlists/$file/
  userguide07.pdf

- Durham County Record Office. Handlist 1. Non-Conformist Church
  Registers
  www.durham.gov.uk/durhamcc/usp.nsf/lookup/pdfhandlists/$file/
  handlist01.pdf

- Durham County Record Office. Handlist 6. Modern Transcripts and Indexes (Non-conformist and Miscellaneous)
www.durham.gov.uk/durhamcc/usp.nsf/lookup/pdfhandlists/$file/
handlist06.pdf

- Parish Register Transcripts and Indexes. Genealogy guide no.5. Newcastle-upon-Tyne Local Studies Library
www.swinhope.demon.co.uk/genuki/NBL/NCLLib/NCLGG5.html
List for Durham and Northumberland

- Parish Registers on Microfilm: Tyne & Wear Archives User Guide 2
www.thenortheast.com/archives/UserGuides/02__ParishRegisters.html

- Cemeteries & Crematoria. Tyne & Wear Archives User Guide 1.
www.thenortheast.com/archives/UserGuides/01__Cemeteries.html
Lists registers, monumental inscriptions, *etc.,* for Gateshead, Newcastle, North Tyneside, South Tyneside and Sunderland

- Transcripts and Indexes. Tyne & Wear Archives User Guide 11.
www.thenortheast.com/archives/UserGuides/11__Transcripts.html
Including many register transcripts *etc.*

- Methodist Registers. Tyne & Wear Archives User Guide 3
www.thenortheast.com/archives/UserGuides/03__Methodist.html

- Records of the Roman Catholic Church. Tyne & Wear Archives User Guide 12
www.thenortheast.com/archives/UserGuides/12__Catholic.html
Birth, marriage and death registers

- Records of the United Reformed Church. Tyne & Wear Archives User Guide 4 (part)
www.thenortheast.com/archives/UserGuides/04__URchurch.html
Birth, marriage and death registers of former Congregational and Presbyterian churches

- Registers of other denominations Tyne & Wear Archives user guide 4 (part)
www.thenortheast.com/archives/UserGuides/04__other.html
Covers Baptist, German Lutheran, Independent Evangelical, Jehovahs Witnesses, Society of Friends, Swedenborgians, and Unitarians

- Tyne & Wear Archives. User Guide 8. Records of the Jewish Community
www.thenortheast.com/archives/UserGuides/08__Jewish.html
Includes information on *Chevra Kadishas* (Jewish burial societies) and cemetery records

- Gateshead Council. Local Studies Department. Miscellaneous Records
www.swinhope.demon.co.uk/genuki/DUR/GatesheadLib/misc.html
Includes list of 'Church records: microfilms & transcripts'; also 'transcriptions of epitaphs and gravestones'.

- Durham
www.sog.org.uk/prc/durham.html
Parish registers, printed, typescript, etc., in the library of the Society of Genealogists

- Durham Parish Registers
www.ndfhs.org.uk/Library/index.html
Click on title. In the library of the Northumberland & Durham Family History Society

- Northumberland & Durham Family History Society. Transcripts on Computer at Bolbec Hall. Part 1: Co. Durham
www.ndfhs.org.uk
Click on title. Parish registers

- Quaker Family History Society: Durham
www.rootsweb.com/~engqfhs/Research/counties/durham.htm
Notes on Quaker records

- Records of the Jewish Community
www.northeast.com/archives/UserGuides/08__Jewish.html
Including cemetery records

Indexes

- A Marriage Database for Northern England (the Joiner Marriage Index)
website.lineone.net/~jjoiner/mindex/mindex.html
Covers 442 parishes in Durham and North Yorkshire

- Brides' Index to the Marriage database for County Durham and the North Riding of Yorkshire (The Joiner Marriage Index)
www.cs.ncl.ac.uk/genuki/Joiner/Brides.html

- Grooms' Index to the Marriage database for County Durham, and the North Riding of Yorkshire. (The Joiner Marriage Index)
  www.cs.ncl.ac.uk/genuki/Joiner/Grooms.html

- Parishes covered by Boyd's Marriage Index: Durham
  www.englishorigins.com/bmi-parishstats.asp?county=Durham

- Genuki / County Durham Search Facility
  www.cs.ncl.ac.uk/genuki/DUR/DURSearch.html
  Database for searching all Durham transcriptions within Genuki held at the University of Newcastle web page

- County Durham Burial Index 1813-1837 (5% sample)
  www.cs.ncl.ac.uk/genuki/Transcriptions/DUR/BDUR.html

- Durham County Record Office Handlist 8: Parishes Indexed on International Genealogical Index and on Boyd's Marriage Index
  www.durham.gov.uk/durhamcc/usp.nsf/lookup/pdfhandlists/$file/handlist08.pdf

- IGI Batch Numbers: Durham Batch Numbers
  freepages.genealogy.rootsweb.com/~tyeroots/durham.html

- IGI Batch Numbers for Durham, England
  freepages.genealogy.rootsweb.com/~hughwallis/IGIBatchNumbers/CountyDurham.htm

Miscellaneous
- Executions at Durham 1732-1909
  www.swinhope.demon.co.uk/genuki/Transcriptions/D__Executions.html

Publications
- Northfiche: Parish Register Transcripts & Indexes: Durham & Cumberland
  www.jwillans.freeserve.co.uk/northfic.html
  Lists of transcripts *etc.,* on fiche for sale

- Original Indexes
  www.original-indexes.demon.co.uk/
  Lists parish registers *etc.,* available on fiche for Co. Durham and Northumberland

Auckland St. Helen
- Marriages from the Auckland St. Helen Registers (1593-1837)
  www.cs.ncl__ac.uk/genuki/Transcriptions/DUR/ASH.html

Aycliffe
- Marriages from the Aycliffe Registers (1560-1837)
  www.cs.ncl.ac.uk/genuki/Transcriptions/DUR/AYC.html

Barnard Castle
- Barnard Castle Baptisms 1813-1837
  www.cs.ncl.ac.uk/genuki/Transcriptions/DUR/XBAR__A-C.html
  Index, continued on 3 further pages

- Barnard Castle Burials 1813-1837
  www.cs.ncl.ac.uk/genuki/Transcriptions/DUR/BBAR__A-K.html
  Index, completed at /BBAR__L-Y.html

Bishop Middleham
- Marriages from the Bishop Middleham Registers (1559-1837)
  www.cs.ncl.ac.uk/genuki/Transcriptions/BMI.html

Bishopton
- Marriages from the Bishopton Registers (1653-1837)
  www.cs.ncl.ac.uk/genuki/Transcriptions/DUR/BIS.html

Bishopwearmouth
- Marriages from the Bishopwearmouth Registers (1813-1823)
  www.cs.ncl.ac.uk/genuki/Transcriptions/DUR/BWM1813.html
  Continued for 1824-31 at /BWM1824.html and for 1832-7 at /BWM1832.html

Boldon
- Marriages from the Boldon Registers (1573-1837)
  www.cs.ncl.ac.uk/genuki/Transcriptions/DUR/BOL.html

Castle Eden
- Marriages from the Castle Eden registers (1698-1837)
  www.cs.ncl.ac.uk/genuki/Transcriptions/DUR/CED.html

Chester le Street
- Marriages from the Chester le Street registers (1582-1699)
  www.cs.ncl.ac.uk/genuki/Transcriptions/DUR/CLS1582.gtml
  Continued as follows:
  1700-1749 /CLS1700.html   1750-1774 /CLS1750.html
  1775-1799 /CLS1775.html   1800-1837 /CLS1800.html

Cockfield
- Cockfield Baptisms 1813-1838
  www.cs.ncl.ac.uk/genuki/Transcriptions/DUR/XCOC.html

- Marriages from the Cockfield Registers (1579-1837)
  www.cs.ncl.ac.uk/genuki/Transcriptions/DUR/COC.html

- Cockfield Burials 1807-1840
  www.cs.ncl.ac.uk/genuki/Transcriptions/DUR/BCOC.html

Cold Hesledon
See Seaham

Coniscliffe
- Marriages from the Coniscliffe Registers (1590-1837)
  www.cs.ncl.ac.uk/genuki/Transcriptions/DUR/CON.html

Croxdale
- Croxdale Baptisms 1813-1893
  www.genuki.org.uk/big/eng/DUR/CroxdaleBap.html

- Marriages from the Croxdale Registers (1732-1837)
  www.cs.ncl.ac.uk/genuki/Transcriptions/DUR/CRO.html

Dalton le Dale
- Marriages from the Dalton le Dale Registers (1653-1837)
  www.cs.ncl.ac.uk/genuki/Transcriptions/DUR/DLD.html
  See also Seaham

Denton
- Marriages from the Denton Registers (1673-1837)
  www.cs.ncl.ac.uk/genuki/Transcriptions/DUR/DEN.html

Durham
- Marriages from the Durham Cathedral Registers (1609-1837)
  www.cs.ncl.ac.uk/genuki/Transcriptions/DUR/DCA.html

- Marriages from the Durham St. Margaret Registers (1558-1739)
  www.cs.ncl.ac.uk/genuki/Transcriptions/DUR/DSM.html
  Continued for 1740-1837 at **/DSM1740.html**

- Marriages from the Durham St. Mary-le-Bow Registers (1571-1837)
  www.cs.ncl.ac.uk/genuki/Transcriptions/DUR/DSB.html

- Marriages from the Durham St. Mary South Bailey Registers (1559-1837)
  www.cs.ncl.ac.uk/genuki/Transcriptions/DUR/DSL.html

- Marriages from the Durham St. Nicholas Registers (1540-1719)
  www.cs.ncl.ac.uk/genuki/Transcriptions/DUR/DSN.html
  Continued for 1720-1837 at **/DSN1720.html**

- Marriages from the Durham St. Oswald Registers (1538-1734)
  www.cs.ncl.ac.uk/genuki/Transcriptions/DUR/DSO.html
  Continued for 1735-1837 at **/DSO1735.html**

Easington
- Marriages from the Easington Registers (1570-1837)
  www.cs.ncl.ac.uk/genuki/Transcriptions/DUR/EAS.html
  See also Seaham

Ebchester
- Marriages from the Ebchester Registers (1619-1837)
  www.cs.ncl.ac.uk/genuki/Transcriptions/DUR/EBC.html

Edmundbyers
- Marriages from the Edmundbyers Registers (1764-1837)
  www.cs.ncl.ac.uk/genuki/Transcriptions/DUR/EDM.html

- Edmundbyers Burials 1813-1837
  www.cs.ncl.ac.uk/genuki/DUR/BEDM.html

Egglescliffe
- Marriages from the Egglescliffe Registers (1540-1837)
  www.cs.ncl.ac.uk/genuki/Transcriptions/DUR/EGG.html

Egglestone
- Egglestone Baptisms 1795-1812
  www.cs.ncl.ac.uk/genuki/Transcriptions/DUR/XEGT1795.html

- Egglestone Baptisms 1813-1837
  www.cs.ncl.ac.uk/genuki/Transcriptions/DUR/XEGT.html

- Egglestone Burials 1796-1840
  www.cs.ncl.ac.uk/genuki/Transcriptions/DUR/BEGT.html

Elwick Hall
- Marriages from the Elwick Hall Registers (1592-1837)
  www.cs.ncl.ac.uk/genuki/Transcriptions/DUR/ELW.html

Embleton
- Marriages from the Embleton Registers (1653-1752)
  www.cs.ncl.ac.uk/genuki/Transcriptions/DUR/EMN.html

Escomb
- Marriages from the Escombe Registers (1543-1837)
  www.cs.ncl.ac.uk/genuki/Transcriptions/DUR/ESC.html

Esh
- Marriages from the Esh Registers (1570-1837)
  www.cs.ncl.ac.uk/genuki/Transcriptions/DUR/ESH.html

Gainford
- Marriages from the Gainford Registers (1569-1719)
  www.cs.ncl.ac.uk/genuki/Transcriptions/DUR/GAI.html
  Continued for 1720-1837 at **/GAI1720.html**

Gateshead
- Marriages from the Gateshead Registers (1558-1837)
  www.cs.ncl.ac.uk/genuki/Transcriptions/DUR/GAT1558.html
  Actually only to 1600 on this page. Continued as follows:
  1600-1699 **/GAT1699.html**   1700-1724 **/GAT1700.html**
  1725-1749 **/GAT1725.html**   1750-1779 **/GAT1750.html**
  1780-1799 **/GAT1780.html**   1800-1819 **/GAT1800.html**
  1820-1837 **/GAT1820.html**

- Victims of the 1854 Fire and Explosion in Gateshead
  www.genuki.org.uk/big/eng/DUR/GreatFire/index.html

Gateshead Fell
- Gateshead Fell Baptisms 1825-1837
  www.cs.ncl.ac.uk/genuki/Transcriptions/DUR/XGAF.html

- Marriages from the Gateshead Fell Registers (1825-1837)
  www.cs.ncl.ac.uk/genuki/Transcriptions/DUR/GAF.html

Great Lumley
- Notebook of Richard Nelson (1825-1911), first sexton of Great Lumley Parish Church
  www.swinhope.demon.co.uk/genuki/Transcriptions/RNelson.htm
  Includes burials and marriages 1866-71

Great Stainton
- Marriages from the Great Stainton registers (1561-1837)
  www.cs.ncl.ac.uk/genuki/Transcriptions/DUR/GST.html

Greatham
- Marriages from the Greatham Registers (1564-1837)
  www.cs.ncl.ac.uk/genuki/Transcriptions/DUR/GRE.html

Grindon
- Marriages from the Grindon registers (1565-1837)
  www.cs.ncl.ac.uk/genuki/Transcriptions/DUR/GRI.html

Hamsterley
- Marriages from the Hamsterley Registers (1580-1837)
  www.cs.ncl.ac.uk/genuki/Transcriptions/DUR/HAM.html

Hawthorn
See Seaham

Heathery Cleugh
- Marriages from the Heathery Cleugh Registers (1828-1837)
  www.cs.ncl.ac.uk/genuki/Transcriptions/DUR/HCL.html

- Heathery Cleugh Burials 1824-1837
  www.cs.ncl.ac.uk/genuki/Transcriptions/DUR/BHCL.html

Heighington
- Marriages from the Heighington Registers (1570-1837)
  www.cs.ncl.ac.uk/genuki/Transcriptions/DUR/HEI.html

Heworth
- Marriages from the Heworth Registers (1696-1774)
  www.cs.ncl.ac.uk/genuki/Transcriptions/DUR/HEW.html
  Continued for 1775-1837 at **/HEW1775.html**

Hetton le Hole
- Marriages from the Hetton-le-Hole Registers (1832-1837)
  www.cs.ncl.ac.uk/genuki/Transcriptions/DUR/HLH.html

Houghton le Spring
- Marriages from the Houghton-le-Spring Registers (1563-1699)
  www.cs.ncl.ac.uk/genuki/Transcriptions/DUR/HSP1563.html
  Continued as follows:
  1700-1749 **/HSP1700.html**   1750-1799 **/HSP1750.html**
  1800-1824 **/HSP1800.html**   1825-1837 **/HSP1825.html**

Hunstanworth
- Marriages from the Hunstanworth Registers (1770-1837)
  www.cs.ncl.ac.uk/genuki/Transcriptions/DUR/HUN.html

- Hunstanworth Burials 1813-1837
  www.cs.ncl.ac.uk/genuki/Transcriptions/DUR/BHUN.html

Hurworth
- Marriages from the Hurworth Registers (1559-1837)
  www.cs.ncl.ac.uk/genuki/Transcriptions/DUR/HUR.html

Jarrow
- Marriages from the Jarrow Registers (1813-1824)
  www.cs.ncl.ac.uk/genuki/Transcriptions/DUR/MJAR1813.html
  Continued for 1825-1837 at /MJAR1825.html

- Marriages from the Registers of Jarrow St. Mark (1896-1948)
  www.cs.ncl.ac.uk/genuki/Transcriptions/DUR/MJARSM.html

- Marriages from the Registers of Jarrow St. Peter (1881-1923)
  www.cs.ncl.ac.uk/genuki/Transcriptions/DUR/MJARSP.html

Jarrow Grange
- Marriages from the Registers of Jarrow Grange Christ Church (1869-1900)
  www.cs.ncl.ac.uk/genuki/Transcriptions/DUR/MJARCC.html

- Marriages from the Registers of Jarrow Grange Good Shepherd (1893-1949)
  www.cs.ncl.ac.uk/genuki/Transcriptions/DUR/MJARGS.html

Kelloe
- Marriages from the Kelloe Registers (1693-1837)
  www.cs.ncl.ac.uk/genuki/Transcriptions/DUR/KEL.html

Lamesley
- Index to Lamesley Baptism Register 1730-1797
  www.cs.ncl.ac.uk/genuki/Transcriptions/DUR/XLAM-AF.html
  Continued at /XLAM-GP.html and /XLAM-RY.html

- Marriages from the Lamesley Registers (1689-1837)
  www.cs.ncl.ac.uk/genuki/Transcriptions/DUR/LAM.html

Long Newton
- Marriages from the Long Newton Registers (1564-1837)
  www.cs.ncl.ac.uk/genuki/Transcriptions/DUR/LON.html

Medomsley
- Marriages from the Medomsley Registers (1608-1837)
  www.cs.ncl.ac.uk/genuki/Transcriptions/DUR/MED.html

Merrington
- Marriages from the Merrington Registers (1579-1837)
  www.cs.ncl.ac.uk/genuki/Transcriptions/DUR/MER.html

Middleton in Teesdale
- Middleton in Teesdale Baptisms 1753-1841
  www.cs.ncl.ac.uk/genuki/Transcriptions/DUR/XMTD__A.html
  Alphabetical index. Continued on 7 further pages

- Middleton in Teesdale Baptisms 1813-1841
  www.cs.ncl.ac.uk/genuki/Transcriptions/DUR/XMTD__A-E.html
  Alphabetical index. Continued on 10 further pages

- Marriages from the Middleton-in-Teesdale Registers (1621-1784)
  www.cs.ncl.ac.uk/genuki/Transcriptions/DUR/MTD.html
  Continued for 1785-1837 at /MTD1785.html

- Middleton in Teesdale Burials 1753-1840
  www.cs.ncl.ac.uk/genuki/Transcriptions/DUR/BMDT-AF.html
  Alphabetical index. Continued at /BMDT-GR.html and /BMDT-SW.html

Middleton St. George
- Marriages from the Middleton St. George Registers (1616-1837)
  www.cs.ncl.ac.uk/genuki/Transcriptions/DUR/MSG.html

Monk Hesledon
- Marriages from the Monk Hesledon Registers (1592-1837)
  www.cs.ncl.ac.uk/genuki/Transcriptions/DUR/MHE.html

Monkwearmouth
- Marriages from the Monkwearmouth Registers (1583-1799)
  www.cs.ncl.ac.uk/genuki/Transcriptions/DUR/MWM1583.html
  Continued as follows:

1800-1812	/MWM1800.html	1813-1826	/MWM1813/html
1825-1837	/MWM1825.html	1827-1837	/MWM1827.html

Muggleswick

- Marriages from the Muggleswick Registers (1755-1837)
  www.cs.ncl.ac.uk/genuki/Transcriptions/DUR/MUG.html

- Marriages from the Registers of Muggleswick (1837-1846)
  www.cs.ncl.ac.uk/genuki/Transcriptions/DUR/MMUG.html

- Muggleswick Burials 1813-1837
  www.cs.ncl.ac.uk/genuki/Transcriptions/DUR/BMUG.html

Murton
See Seaham

New Seaham
See Seaham

Old Seaham
See Seaham

Penshaw

- Marriages from the Penshaw Registers (1754-1837)
  www.cs.ncl.ac.uk/genuki/Transcriptions/DUR/PEN.html

Pittington

- Marriages from the Pittington Registers (1575-1837)
  www.cs.ncl.ac.uk/genuki/Transcriptions/DUR/PIT.html

Redmarshall

- Marriages from the Redmarshall Registers (1560-1837)
  www.cs.ncl.ac.uk/genuki/Transcriptions/DUR/RED.html

Ryton

- Marriages from the Ryton Registers (1581-1699)
  www.cs.ncl.ac.uk/genuki/Transcriptions/DUR/RYT1581.html
  Continued as follows:
  1700-1749 /RYT1700.html   1750-1779 /RYT1750.html
  1780-1812 /RYT1780.html   1800-1837 /RYT1800.html
  1813-1837 /RYT1813.html

Satley

- Marriages from the Satley Registers (1560-1837)
  www.cs.ncl.ac.uk/genuki/Transcriptions/DUR/SAT.html

Seaham

- Seaham Super Index
  dspace.dial.pipex.com/town/street/kch66/index.html
  Fee-based index to parish registers and other records for Old Seaham, New Seaham, Seaham Harbour, Seaton, Dalton-le-Dale, Cold Hesledon, Murton, Hawthorn and Easington. More places are being added

- Marriages from the Seaham Registers (1652-1837)
  www.cs.ncl.ac.uk/genuki/Transcriptions/DUR/SEA.html

Seaton
See Seaham

Sedgefield

- Marriages from the Sedgefield Registers (1581-1729)
  www.cs.ncl.ac.uk/genuki/Transcriptions/DUR/SED.html
  Continued for 1730-1837 at /SED1730.html

Sherburn Hospital

- Marriages from the Sherburn Hospital Registers (1695-1837)
  www.cs.ncl.ac.uk/genuki/Transcriptions/DUR/SHO.html

Shildon

- Marriages from the Shildon Registers (1834-1837)
  www.cs.ncl.ac.uk/genuki/Transcriptions/DUR/SHI.html

Sockburn

- Marriages from the Sockburn Registers (1580-1837)
  www.cs.ncl.ac.uk/genuki/Transcriptions/DUR/SOC.html

South Shields

- Marriages from the Registers of South Shields St. Aiden (1888-1910)
  www.cs.ncl.ac.uk/genuki/Transcriptions/DUR/MSSHSA.html

- Marriages from the South Shields St. Hilda Registers (1653-1699)
  www.cs.ncl.ac.uk/genuki/Transcriptions/DUR/SSH1653.html
  Continued as follows:
  1700-1749 /SSH1700.html   1750-1779 /SSH1750.html
  1780-1799 /SSH1780.html   1800-1812 /SSH1800.html
  1813-1824 /SSH1813.html   1825-1837 /SSH1825.html

- Marriages from the Registers of South Shields, St. Hilda (1837-1844)
  www.cs.ncl.ac.uk/genuki/Transcriptions/DUR/MSSH1837.html
  Continued as follows:
  1845-1850 **/MSSH1845.html**   1851-1858   **/MSSH1851.html**
  1859-1868 **/MSSH1859.html**   1869-1880   **/MSSH1869.html**
  1881-1901 **/MSSH1881.html**

- Marriages from the Registers of South Shields St. Jude (1886-1914)
  www.cs.ncl.ac.uk/genuki/Transcriptions/DUR/MSSHSJ.html

- Marriages from the Registers of South Shields St. Michael (1882-1889)
  www.cs.ncl.ac.uk/genuki/Transcriptions/DUR/MSSHSM1882.html
  Continued for 1900-1908 at **/MSSHSM1900.html**

- South Shields Society of Friends: Burials 1673-1697
  www.cs.ncl.ac.uk/genuki/Transcriptions/DUR/BSSH-SoF.html
  From *Archaeologia Aeliana* N.S. **16**(1), 1894

Spennymoor
- Derek Boy's Index to Marriage Registers of St. Paul's, Spennymoor, 1863-1914
  www.cs.ncl.ac.uk/genuki/Transcriptions/DUR/SpennyA-J.html
  Continued on 1 further page

Staindrop
- Staindrop Baptisms 1813-1838
  www.cs.ncl.ac.uk/genuki/Transcriptions/DUR/XSTD__A-J.html
  Alphabetical index. Continued at **/XSTD__K-Y.html**

- Marriages from the Staindrop Registers (1626-1764)
  www.cs.ncl.ac.uk/genuki/Transcriptions/DUR/STD.html
  Continued for 1765-1837 at **/STD1765.html**

- Staindrop Burials 1813-1840
  www.cs.ncl.ac.uk/genuki/Transcriptions/DUR/BSTD.html
  Indexed (from 1807) at **/BSTD__AK.html**
  and **/BSTD__LY.html**

Stanhope
- Marriages from the Stanhope Registers (1613-1749)
  www.cs.ncl.ac.uk/genuki/Transcriptions/DUR/STP1613.html
  Continued as follows:
  1750-1799 **/STP1750.html**   1800-1837 **/STP1800.html**

- Stanhope Burial Register 1854-1905
  www.cs.ncl.ac.uk/genuki/Transcriptions/DUR/BSTP-AG.html
  Continued on 2 further pages

Stockton on Tees
- Stockton on Tees Baptisms 1637-1780
  www.cs.ncl.ac.uk/genuki/Transcriptions/DUR/XSTO__A-B.html
  Continued on 6 further pages. Alphabetical index.

- Stockton St. James 1868-1910
  homepages.rootsweb.com/~mwi/stockton.txt
  Marriages

Sunderland
- Marriages from the Sunderland Registers (1719-1749)
  www.cs.ncl.ac.uk/genuki/Transcriptions/DUR/SUN1719.html
  Continued as follows:
  1750-1764 **/SUN1750.html**   1765-1774   **/SUN1765.html**
  1775-1784 **/SUN1775.html**   1785-1799   **/SUN1785.html**
  1800-1814 **/SUN1800.html**   1815-1824   **/SUN1815.html**
  1825-1829 **/SUN1825.html**   1830-1837   **/SUN1830.html**

- Victims of the Victoria Hall Calamity
  www.swinhope.demon.co.uk/genuki/Transcriptions/VictoriaHall.html
  Lists victims of a Sunderland tragedy in 1883

Trimdon
- Marriages from the Trimdon Registers (1720-1837)
  www.cs.ncl.ac.uk/genuki/Transcriptions/DUR/TRI.html

Washington
- Marriages from the Washington Registers (1603-1837)
  www.cs.ncl.ac.uk/genuki/Transcriptions/DUR/WAS.html

Weardale St. John
- Marriages from the St. John's Chapel (Weardale) Registers (1828-1837)
  www.cs.ncl.ac.uk/genuki/Transcriptions/DUR/SJC.html
  See also Wolsingham

West Baldon
- West Boldon Society of Friends Burials 1657-1682
  www.cs.ncl.ac.uk/genuki/Transcriptions/DUR/BBOL-Sof.html
  From *Archaeologia Aeliana* N.S. **16**(1), 1894

West Rainton

- Marriages from the West Rainton Registers (1827-1837)
  www.cs.ncl.ac.uk/genuki/Transcriptions/DUR/WRA.html

Whickham

- Marriages from the Whickham Registers (1534-1654)
  www.cs.ncl.ac.uk/genuki/Transcriptions/DUR/WHK1579.html
  Continued as follows:
  1655-1724 /WHK1655.html   1725-1774 /WHK1725.html
  1775-1812 /WHK1775.html   1813-1837 /WHK1813.html

Whitburn

- Whitburn Baptisms 1813-1839
  www.cs.ncl.ac.uk/genuki/Transcriptions/DUR/XWBN.html

- Marriages from the Whitburn Registers (1579-1837)
  www.cs.ncl.ac.uk/genuki/Transcriptions/DUR/WBN.html

Whitworth

- Marriages from the Whitworth Registers 1754-1837
  www.cs.ncl.ac.uk/genuki/Transcriptions/DUR/MWHW.html

Whorlton

- Whorlton Baptisms 1841-1899
  www.cs.ncl.ac.uk/genuki/Transcriptions/DUR/XWHO.html

- Marriages from the Whorlton Registers (1713-1837)
  www.cs.ncl.ac.uk/genuki/Transcriptions/DUR/WHO.html

- Whorlton Burials 1813-1899
  www.cs.ncl.ac.uk/genuki/Transcriptions/DUR/BWHO.html

Winlaton

- Marriages from the Winlaton Registers (1833-1837)
  www.cs.ncl.ac.uk/genuki/Transcriptions/DUR/MWinlaton.html

Winston

- Winston Baptisms 1813-1840
  www.cs.ncl.ac.uk/genuki/Transcriptions/DUR/XWIS.html

- Marriages from the Winston Registers (1716-1837)
  www.cs.ncl.ac.uk/genuki/Transcriptions/DUR/WIS.html

- Winston Burials 1814-1840
  www.cs.ncl.ac.uk/genuki/Transcriptions/DUR/BWIS.html

Witton Gilbert

- Marriages from the Witton Gilbert Registers (1568-1837)
  www.cs.ncl.ac.uk/genuki/Transcriptions/DUR/WIT.html

Witton le Wear

- Marriages from the Witton le Wear Registers (1558-1837)
  www.cs.ncl.ac.uk/genuki/Transcriptions/DUR/WLW.html

Wolsingham

- Wolsingham and Weardale Chapel Baptisms 1813-1827
  website.lineone.net/~pjoiner/genuki/DUR/Wolsingham/WOL.html

Essex

Civil Registration
- Registration Districts in Essex
  www.fhsc.org.uk/genuki/reg/ess.htm
  Between 1837 and 1930

- St. Catherine's Index of Marriages, October/November/December 1839: [Essex and S. Suffolk]
  www.cs.ncl.ac.uk/genuki/StCathsTranscriptions/CATHPRS9.TXT
  Continued on 7 further pages

- [St. Catherine's House Marriage Index, Jan-March, 1849. District 12. Essex/South Suffolk]
  www.cs.ncl.ac.uk/genuki/StCathsTranscriptions/CP491__12.TXT

- St. Catherine's marriages 1856/Q1. Volumes 4a and 4b
  www.cs.ncl.ac.uk/genuki/StCathsTranscriptions/CATH56/CTH56104.TXT
  Covers Essex, Suffolk and Norfolk, January-March 1856

Parish & Non-Parochial Registers: Introductory Pages & Lists
- Essex
  www.sog.org.uk/prc/ess.html
  Parish registers, printed, typescript, *etc.,* in the library of the Society of Genealogists

- Quaker Family History Society: Essex
  www.rootsweb.com/~engqfhs/Research/counties/essex.htm
  Notes on Quaker records

Indexes
- Essex Baptism Index 1780-1840
  www.nivek-systems.co.uk/genuki/ESS/ESS.baptisms.html

- Marriages
  www.nivek-systems.co.uk/genuki/ESS/ESS.marriages.html
  Notes on Essex marriage indexes

- Parishes covered by Boyd's Marriage Index: Essex
  www.englishorigins.com/bmi-parishstats.asp?county=Essex

- Some Marriage Entries from Boyd's Index for Essex
  freepages.genealogy.rootsweb.com/~boydsindex/Boydsindex.htm

- Essex burials 1813-1865
  www.nivek-systems.co.uk/genuki/ESS/ESS.burials.html
  Index

- IGI Batch Numbers: Essex Batch Numbers
  freepages.genealogy.rootsweb.com/~tyeroots/essex.html

- IGI Batch Numbers for Essex, England
  freepages.genealogy.rootsweb.com/~hughwallis/IGIBatchNumbers/
  CountyEssex.htm

Transcript Collections on the Web
- Essex Villages
  www.essexvillages.net

Publications
- The East of London Family History Society: Parish Register Indexes and Guides
  eolfhs.rootsweb.com/pubprig.htm
  Booklets and fiche relating to Essex and Middlesex for sale

Beaumont
- An Index to the Registers of Beaumont, Essex, U.K.
  www.essexpast.co.uk/beaumont/bmntintro.html
  Based on Crisp's transcript published in 1899

Haverhill
- Haverhill Cemetery Burial Records
  www.haverhill-uk.com/genealogy/cemetery/index.shtml
  Searchable database, 1867-1950

Kelvedon Hatch
- Kelvedon Hatch, Essex: Local and Family History: From the Registers of St. Nicholas's Church: Marriages 1837-1898
  www.historyhouse.co.uk/marriages__1837__1898.html

- Kelvedon Hatch, Essex: Local and Family History: From the Registers of St. Nicholas's Church: burials 1813-1897
  www.historyhouse.co.uk/burials__1813__1898.html

Mount Bures
- Mount Bures
  mysite.freeserve.com/Mountbures
  Baptisms 1668-1751 & 1818-39; marriages 1668-1751 & 1791-1823; burials 1668-1751 & 1786-1957. Continued at **/Mount-Bures2**

Steeple Bumpstead
- Steeple Bumpstead: indexes and transcriptions
  **www.essexvillages.net/essex/steeplebumpstead/indexes/
  sbumpsteadindexes.html**
  Index of baptisms, 1676-1907

Stisted
- Stisted Indexes & Transcriptions
  www.essexvillages.net/essex/stistedindexes.html
  Lookups offered

Wakes Colne
- Wakes Colne
  mysite.freeserve.com/www.colnedatabase.co
  Marriages 1694-1700, 1755-1809 & 1870-9; baptisms 1869-92 & 1921-4; burials 1813-87

Hertfordshire

Civil Registration
- Registration Districts in Hertfordshire
  www.fhsc.org.uk/genuki/reg.hrt.htm
  Between 1837 and 1930

Parish & Non-Parochial Registers: Introductory Pages and Lists
- Local and Family History on Herts Direct: Parish Registers
  www.hertsdirect.org/infoadvice/history/whatgot/parishregisters/
  Includes down-loadable lists of registers in Hertfordshire libraries and archives

- Local and Family History on Herts Direct: Non-conformist Registers
  www.hertsdirect.org/infoadvice/history/whotgot/nonconformistregs/
  Includes downloadable list of registers at Hertforshire Archives Local Studies

- Hertfordshire
  www.sog.org.uk/prc/hertfordshire.html
  Parish registers, printed, typescript, *etc.,* in the library of the Society of Genealogists

- Quaker Family History Society: Hertfordshire
  www.rootsweb.com/~engqfhs/Research/counties/hertford.htm
  Notes on Quaker records

Indexes
- IGI Batch Numbers: Hertfordshire Batch Numbers
  freepages.genealogy.rootsweb.com/~tyeroots/hertford.html

- IGI Batch Numbers for Hertford, England
  **freepages.genealogy.rootsweb.com/~hughwallis/IGIBatchNumbers/
  CountyHertford.htm**

Lookups
- Hertfordshire Look Ups
  homepage.ntlworld.com/thehaunt/hertford.htm
  Look-ups of parish registers, monumental inscriptions *etc.* offered

Bovingdon
- Transcribed documents relating to Bovingdon, Hertfordshire
  www.geocities.com/mellowsbrown/tranlist.html
  Lookups offered in the parish registers, monumental inscriptions *etc.*

Little Munden
- 17th and 18th century Little Munden parish records
  www.mundens.net/genealogy/lmrecords.htm
  Brief note

- Names found in Little Munden Parish Records
  www.mundens.net/genealogy/lmnames.htm

Huntingdonshire

Civil Registration
- Registration Districts in Huntingdon
  www.fhsc.org.uk/genuki/reg/hun.htm
  Between 1837 and 1930

Parish & Non-Parochial Registers: Introductory Pages & Lists
- Summary of Documentary and Library Holdings in the Huntingdon County Record Office
  www.genuki.org.uk/big/eng/HUN/RecordOffice.html
  Includes brief notes on registers *etc.*
- Microfilm Holdings of Parish Registers & Bishops Transcripts at the County Record Office, Huntingdon
  www.genuki.org.uk/big/eng/CAM/HuntingdonRecordOfficeMicrofilm Holdings.html
- Huntingdonshire
  www.sog.org.uk/prc/huntingdonshire.html
  Parish registers, printed, typescript, *etc.,* in the library of the Society of Genealogists
- Quaker Family History Society: Huntingdonshire
  www.rootsweb.com/~engqfhs/Research/counties/hunts.htm
  Notes on Quaker records

Indexes
- IGI Batch Numbers: Huntingdonshire Batch Numbers
  freepages.genealogy.rootsweb.com/~tyeroots/huntingdon.html
- IGI Batch Numbers for Huntingdon, England
  freepages.genealogy.rootsweb.com/~hughwallis/IGIBatchNumbers/ CountyHuntingdon.htm

Publications
- Huntingdonshire Family History Society bookstall
  www.hunts.fhs.org.uk/Pubs.html
  Includes many parish registers, monumental inscriptions, *etc.* for sale

Winwick
- Winwick Parish Register Extracts
  freepages.genealogy.rootsweb.com/~maureenbryson/id65.htm
  Selected surnames only

Isle of Man

Parish & Non-Parochial Registers; Introductory Pages & Lists
See also Cumberland

- Parish Records
  www.isle-of-man.com/manxnotebook/famhist/genealgy/church.htm
  Isle of Man registers

- Isle of Man
  www.sog.org.uk/prc/iom.html
  Parish registers, printed, typescript, *etc.,* in the library of the Society of Genealogists

- Quaker Family History Society: Isle of Man
  www.rootsweb.com/~engqfhs/Research/counties/man.htm
  Notes on Quaker records

Indexes
- IGI Batch Numbers for Isle of Man, England
  freepages.genealogy.rootsweb.com/~hughwallis/IGIBatchNumbers/
  Countylsle__of__Man.htm

Publications
- Isle of Man Family History Society Publications
  www.isle-of-man.com/interests/genealogy/fhs/fhspub.shtml
  Includes burial registers *etc.*

Ballaugh
- Notes from the Registers: the Parish of Ballaugh
  www.isle-of-man.com/manxnotebook/manxnb/v02p055.htm
  Brief extracts only

Braddon
- Parish of Braddan
  www.isle-of-man.com/manxnotebook/parishes/bn/regs.htm
  Brief extracts from the parish register

German
- Extract from German Vestry Book
  www.isle-of-man.com/manxnotebook/parishes/gn/preg.htm
  Includes brief notes on burials

Kirk Michael
- Notes on the Parish Registers of Kirk Michael, Isle of Mann
  www.isle-of-man.com/manxnotebook/iomnhas/lm1p003.htm
  Brief discussion

Kirk Onchan
- The Kirk Onchan Registers
  www.isle-of-man.com/manxnotebook/parishes/on/onreg.htm
  Brief discussion with extracts

Lezayre
- Extracts from Lezayre Parish Registers
  www.isle-of-man.com/manxnotebook/parishes/le/regs.htm
  Covers 1696-1709

Lonan
- The Parish of Lonan
  www.isle-of-man.com/manxnotebook/parishes/lnreg.htm
  Brief notes from the register

Malew
- Notes from the Registers: the Parish of Malew
  www.isle-of-man.com/manxnotebook/manxnb/v06p072.htm
  Brief extracts

Marown
- Extracts from the Parish Register
  www.isle-of-man.com/manxnotebook/parishes/mn/pr.htm
  Of Marown. Brief

Maughold
- The Parish of Maughold
  www.isle-of-man.com/manxnotebook/parishes/md/mdreg.htm
  Brief extracts from the parish register

Rushen
- Rushen Parish Church, with extracts from old parish books
  www.isle-of-man.com/manxnotebook/parishes/rn/preg.htm
  Brief discussion with extracts

Santan
- Santan Parish Registerssss
  www.isle-of-man.com/manxnotebook/parishes/sn/preg.htm
  Baptisms 1690-1717; burials 1656-1850. Incomplete?

Lancashire

Civil Registration
- Registration Districts in Lancashire
  www.fhsc.org.uk/genuki/reg/lan.htm
  Between 1837 and 1930

- [St. Catherine's House Marriage Index, Jan-March, 1849. District 20. Lancashire]
  www.cs.ncl.ac.uk/genuki/StCathsTranscriptions/CATH4920.TXT

- [St. Catherine's House Marriage Index, Jan-March, 1849. District 21. Lancashire]
  www.cs.ncl.ac.uk/genuki/StCathsTranscriptions/CATH4921.TXT

- Unwanted BMD Certificates: Liverpool & SW Lancs Family History Society
  freepages.genealogy.rootsweb.com/~lswlfhs/certs.htm

Parish & Non-Parochial Registers: Introductory Pages & Lists
- Lancashire County Library: Library Services: Local Studies: Parish Registers
  www.lancashire.gov.uk/libraries/services/local/parish.asp
  Brief introduction

- Knowsley Library Service: Parish Registers
  www.knowsley.gov.uk/leisure/libraries/services/localhistory/parish.html
  List of published registers held (including fiche)

- Records of Roman Catholic Churches held at the Liverpool Record Office
  freepages.genealogy.rootsweb.com/~hibernia/rchurchrec.html

- Roman Catholic Registers on Microfilm at the Liverpool Record Office
  freepages.genealogy.rootsweb.com/~hibernia/rcrom.htm

- Oldham Local Studies and Archives: Parish Registers
  www.oldham.gov.uk/leisure/local__studies/parish.shtml

- Lancashire
  www.sog.org.uk/prc/lan.html
  Parish registers, printed, typescript, *etc.,* in the library of the Society of Genealogists

- Quaker Family History Society: Lancashire
  www.rootsweb.com/~engqfhs/Research/counties/lancs.htm
  Notes on Quaker records

Indexes
- Parishes covered by Boyd's Marriage Index: Lancashire
  www.englishorigins.com/bmi-parishstats.asp?county=Lancashire

- IGI Batch Numbers for Lancashire, England
  freepages.genealogy.rootsweb.com/~hughwallis/IGIBatchNumbers/
  CountyLancashire__(A-K).htm
  Continued at **/CountyLancashire__(L-O).htm** and **/CountyLancashire__(P-Z).htm**

- IGI Batch Numbers: Lancashire Batch Numbers
  freepages.genealogy.rootsweb.com/~tyeroots/lanc.html

Publications
- The Lancashire Parish Register Society
  www.genuki.org.uk/big/eng/LAN/lprs/
  Includes list of printed registers

- Lancashire Parish Register Society
  www.mlfhs.demon.co.uk/Bookshop/index.html
  List of registers currently available from the bookshop of the Manchester & Lancashire Family History Society

- Lancashire Family History and Heraldry Society: Current Microfiche Publications
  www.lancashire-fhhs.org.uk/pubs-f.htm
  Includes many parish registers

- Microfiche Publications: Liverpool & S.W. Lancs Family History Society
  freepages.genealogy.rootsweb.com/~lswlfhs/Microfichepub.htm
  Parish registers on fiche

- Manchester & Lancashire F.H.S. Bookshop
www.mlfhs.demon.co.uk/Bookshop/index.html
Click on 'our publications'. List of the Society's publications, including many parish registers and monumental inscriptions.

- [North Meols Family History Society]: Publications for Sale
www.users.zetnet.co.uk/nmfhs/pages/pubs.htm
Includes many parish register extracts on fiche etc.

Barton on Irwell
- Barton Wesleyan Chapel Burials
www.mancuniensis.btinternet.co.uk/BWCBFP.htm
1804-1902, in progress

Bolton le Moors
- The Bolton Parish Church Burials
homepages.rootsweb.com/~surnamru/boltonburi.html
For 1854 only

Charlestown
See Pendleton

Farnworth
See Prescot

Garston
See Grassendale

Grassendale
- Baptisms, St. Austin's RC Church, Grassendale, Garston, Liverpool, 1856-1882
freepages.genealogy.rootsweb.com/~hibernia/ausbp.htm

Great Carlton
- Great Carlton Transcriptions
www.wparkinson.com/Great%20Carlton.htm
Baptisms 1813-1978; marriages 1813-37

Great Crosby
- Burials. Ss. Peter & Paul's R.C. Church, Great Crosby, near Liverpool
freepages.genealogy.rootsweb.com/~hibernia/sspp/sspp.htm
Index, 19th c.

Great Sankey
See Prescot

Greengate
- Greengate Unitarian Baptisms 1825-1837
www.salfordroots.com/GreengateUnitarianChapelBaptisms1825-1837Indexed.htm

- Greengate Unitarian Meeting House Burial Register 1826-1837
www.salfordroots.com/GreengateUnitBurs1826-1837Indexed.htm

Kirkdale
- St. Mary's Church, Kirkdale, Liverpool: marriages extracted from LDS film#1545938, covering the period from 4th October 1874 to 11th December 1883
homepages.rootsweb.com/~mwi/liverpool.txt
Also at
www.genuki.org.uk/big/eng/LAN/Liverpool/St.Mary-marr-1874-1883.txt

Little Carlton
- Little Carlton Transcriptions
www.wparkinson.com/Little%20Carlton.htm
Baptisms 1813-1978; marriages 1813-37

Little Crosby
- Little Crosby Church, St Mary's
www.sunnyfields.freeserve.co.uk/church/
Includes baptisms 1801-56; marriages 1835-56; deaths 1812-56 and monumental inscriptions

Liverpool
See also Grassendale

- Liverpool Area R.C. Marriage Index Home Page
freepages.genealogy.rootsweb.com/~hibernia/mar/mar.htm
Index of 64,000 names of the 19th c.

- Liverpool Marriages and Obituaries
freepages.genealogy.rootsweb.com/~liverpool/main.html
From the *Liverpool Mercury*, 1811-34; also includes other information from Liverpool newspapers

Manchester
- Family History in Manchester
  www.manchester.gov.uk/libraries/arls/famhist.htm
  Includes notes on 'Church of England Registers', 'Non-conformist, Catholic and Jewish Records', and 'Cemetery records and Monumental Inscriptions' at Manchester Public Library
- Manchester Church History
  www.genuki.org.uk/big/eng/LAN/Manchester/church_history.html
  Includes brief notes on registers, and on 'the reasons for marriage in the Cathedral'.

Mellor
- St. Thomas's Parish Church, Mellor
  freepages.genealogy.rootsweb.com/~dusk/mellor_pr.html
  Includes selected baptisms 1631-1914; marriages 1839-1926 (Higginbottom only) and burials 1624-1918; also Phillimore's published marriage transcript, 1678-1775.

New Windsor
See Salford

Pendleton
- Salford, Pendleton Methodist New Connexion, Baptisms, 1813-1837
  www.salfordroots.com/MethNewConnexion1813-1837Indexedbaptisms.htm
- Baptisms at the Independent Chapel, Charlestown, Pendleton 1836-1837
  www.salfordroots.com/CharlestownIndBaptisms1836-1837.htm

Prescot
- Summary Location List for Christenings Marriages & Burials
  prescotchurch.merseyworld.com/records.html
  For Prescot, Farnworth, Rainford Chapel, St. Helen's and Great Sankey

Rainford Chapel
See Prescot

St. Helen's
See Prescot

Salford
- Salford Parish Transcriptions
  www.salfordroots.com/page8.htm
  Collection of transcripts, separately listed here
- Brunswick Chapel Baptisms 1814-1837
  www.salfordroots.com/Brunswickchapelbaptisms1814-1837Indexed.htm
- Chapel St. Independent Baptisms 1820-1834
  www.salfordroots.com/Chapelstindbaptismxtra.htm
  Index
- Salford, Christ Church, King Street, Bible Christians: Baptisms in Burial Register
  www.salfordroots.com/BaptismsinBurialRegisterChristChKSBCA-B.htm
  Continued on 4 further pages
- Salford, Christ Church, King Street Bible Christians Burials 1800
  www.salfordroots.com/1800ChristChKSBCBurialsIndexed.htm
  Continued to 1811 on 32 further pages
- Salford New Windsor Baptisms 1800-1837
  www.salfordroots.com/SalfordNewWindsorBaptisms1800-1837INDEXED.htm
  Index
- Salford New Windsor Burials 1800-1837
  www.salfordroots.com/NewWindsorBurials1800-1837INDEXED.htm

Leicestershire

Civil Registration
* Registration Districts in Leicestershire
  www.fhsc.org.uk/genuki/reg/lei.htm
  Between 1837 and 1930

* [St. Catherine's House Marriage Index, Jan-March, 1849. District 15. Leicestershire/Nottinghamshire
  www.cs.ncl.ac.uk/genuki/StCathsTranscriptions/CATH4915.TXT

Parish & Non-Parochial Registers: Introductory Pages & Lists
* Leicestershire Libraries and Information Service: Census returns and parish registers in Leicestershire Libraries
  www.leics.gov.uk/libraries/local_studies/

* Leicestershire
  www.sog.org.uk/prc/leicester.html
  Parish registers, printed, typescript, *etc.,* in the library of the Society of Genealogists

* Quaker Family History Society: Leicestershire & Rutland
  www.rootsweb.com/~engqfhs/Research/counties/leics.htm
  Notes on Quaker records

Indexes
* Marriage Database
  www.uk-genealogy.org.uk/datafiles/marriagesearch.html
  Index to various registers, especially in Leicestershire and the East Midlands

* Free Reg: Leicestershire
  freereg.rootsweb.com/parishes/lei/index.htm
  Details of the registers currently included in a project to index births, deaths and marriages

* IGI Batch Numbers: Leicestershire Batch Numbers
  freepages.genealogy.rootsweb.com/~tyeroots/leicester.html

* IGI Batch Numbers for Leicester, England
  freepages.genealogy.rootsweb.com/~hughwallis/IGIBatchNumbers/
  CountyLeicester.htm

Publications
* Leicestershire & Rutland Family History Society: Society Publications
  lrfhs.org.uk/publications.html
  Includes parish registers, monumental inscriptions, *etc.*

Appleby
* Village Families: Inhabitants of Appleby, 1560-1701
  www.applebymagna.org.uk/appleby_history/
  villagers_early_modern_inhabitants.htm
  List of surnames from the parish register, probate records, etc.

Bottesford
* Bottesford Parish Records
  freespace.virgin.net/guy.etchells/Botprindex.htm
  Marriages, 1563-1812

Desford
* Desford
  www.uk-genealogy.org.uk/cgi-bin/marriagedb.pl
  Search 'Desford'. Marriages 1559-1837

Eastwell
* Eastwell Parish Records
  freespace.virgin.net/guy.etchells/Eastprindex.htm
  Marriages, 1588-1749 and 1754-1832

Hoton
* Hoton Parish Records: Marriages 1654 to 1826
  freespace.virgin.net/guy.etchells/Hoton.htm
  Transcription

Leicester
* St. Margaret's Marriage Index
  www.geocities.com/Heartland/Pond/1598/stmargs.html
  Index to a Leicester church register, 1837-97

Long Clawson
* Long Clawson Parish Records
  freespace.virgin.net/guy.etchells/LCprindex.htm
  Marriages 1558-1921; burials 1748-1769

Muston
* Muston Parish Records
  freespace.virgin.net/guy.etchells/MUprindex.htm
  Marriages 1562-1812

Netherseal
- Parish & Non-Conformist Registers
freepages.genealogy.rootsweb.com/~brett/seal.htm#Parish
List of registers, transcripts, films *etc.,* for Netherseal and Overseal

Overseal
See Netherseal

Peckleton
- Peckleton
www.uk-genealogy.org.uk/cgi-bin/marriagedb.pl
Search 'Peckleton'. Marriages 1567-1763

Quorndon
- Quorndon Parish Records
freespace.virgin.net/guy/etchells/Quprindex.htm
Marriages 1576-1837

Ratcliffe Culey
- Marriages
www.mdlp.co.uk/resources/ratcliffe/marriages/rcm%20frames.htm
At Ratcliffe Culey, 1754-1995. Indexes only
- All Saints, Ratcliffe Culey burial transcription
www.mdlp.co.uk/resources/ratcliffe/Burials%20Frames/
Burials%20Frames.htm
1710-1995

Sheepy Magna
- Sheepy Magna Burials
www.mdlp.co.uk/resources/Sheepy/Display%20Burials/
Burials%20Frame.htm
Index, 1710-1995, with related monumental inscriptions

Sibson
- Sibson
www.mdlp.co.uk/resources/Sibson/index.htm
Burials from the parish register; forthcoming

Thringstone
- St Andrews, Thringstone: from the parish registers
www.geocities.com/oliveshark53/StAndreg.htm

Wartnaby
- Wartnaby Parish Records: Marriages 1635 to 1838
freespace.virgin.net/guy.etchells/Wart.htm

Lincolnshire

Civil Registration
- Registration Districts in Lincolnshire
www.fhsc.org.uk/genuki/reg/lin.htm
Between 1837 and 1930

- Civil Registration
www.genuki.org.uk/big/eng/LIN/civilreg.html
www.rootsweb.com/~englin/civilreg.htm
On the Lincolnshire Genuki and Genweb pages, but of general as well as Lincolnshire interest

- Lincolnshire Registration Service: Births, Deaths and Marriages
www.lincolnshire.gov.uk/lccconnect/socialservices/RegService/home.htm

Parish & Non-Parochial Registers: Introductory Pages & Lists
- Lincolnshire Church and Parish Records
www.genuki.org.uk/big/eng/LIN/churchrecs.html
www.rootsweb.com/~englin/churchrecs.htm
Introductory page from Genuki and Genweb

- Deposited Parish Registers and Bishops Transcripts
www.lincolnshire.gov.uk/lccconnect/cultural/services/archives/
Family/ParishReg.htm
At Lincolnshire Archives

- Lincolnshire Non-Conformist Records
www.genuki.org.uk/big/eng/LIN/nonconformist.html
Introductory page from Genuki

- Guide to Sources: Records of Non-conformist Denominations
www.lincolnshire.gov.uk/lccconnect/culturalservices/archives/
Sources/Nonconformist.htm
At Lincolnshire Archives

- Marriage Indexes
www.nelincs.gov.uk/IC/noframes/living/library/marrindex.htm
Published indexes held at North East Lincolnshire Local Studies Library

- Lincolnshire
  www.sog.org.uk/prc/lin.html
  Parish registers, printed, typescripts, *etc.,* in the library of the Society of Genealogists

- Quaker Family History Society: Lincolnshire
  www.rootsweb.com/~engqfhs/Research/counties/lincs.htm
  Notes on Quaker records

Indexes

- Parish Registers
  www.srichards.freeserve.co.uk/genealo-parishregisters.htm
  Index of Lincolnshire baptisms, marriages and burials for selected parishes and names

- IGI Batch Numbers: Lincolnshire Batch Numbers
  freepages.genealogy.rootsweb.com/~tyeroots/lincoln.html

- IGI Batch Numbers for Lincoln, England
  freepages.genealogy.rootsweb.com/~hughwallis/
  IGIBatchNumbers/CountyLincoln__(A-J).htm
  Continued at
  /CountyLincoln__(K-R).htm and /CountyLincoln__(S-Z).htm

Publications

- Lincolnshire Family History Society: Marriages
  www.genuki.org.uk/big/eng/LIN/lfhs/Publications/Pubsmarr.htm
  Indexes in fiche or book format for sale

- Lincolnshire Family History Society: Burial Indexes
  www.genuki.org.uk/big/eng/LIN/lfhs/Publications/PubsBurails.htm
  Fiche publications

- The Isle of Axholme Family History Society Publications List
  www.linktop.demon.co.uk/axholme/order.htm
  Includes many parish registers

- The Isle of Axholme: Marriage Index Database Programme
  www.linktop.demon.co.uk/axholme/advert.htm
  Details of a database for sale on floppy disks

Bottesford

- Bottesford Parish Marriages: 1745 to 1772
  freespace.virgin.net/guy.etchells/Botpr6.htm

Crowle

- Crowle Parish Register Extracts
  freepages.genealogy.rootsweb.com/~maureenbryson/id54.htm
  Selected surnames only ·

Great Carlton

- Great Carlton Transcriptions
  www.wparkinson.com/Great%20Carlton.htm
  Baptisms 1813-1978; marriages 1813-37

Grimsby

- Grimsby Marriage Records
  www.zah.ndirect.co.uk/marriagedbase.htm
  Marriages of Grimsby Hebrew Community, 1876-1972

Holbeach

- Holbeach Parish Registers
  www.pcug.org.au/~bthompso/holbeach/readme.htm
  Scanned transcript of a register originally published 1892.

Langton by Partney

- Langton by Partney Burials commencing 1761
  www.genuki.org.uk/big/eng/LIN/LangtonPartney/
  langtonpartney__register.txt

  To 1812

North Hykeham

- North Hykeham Parish Registers
  www.wparkinson.com/Hykeham/nhpage.htm
  Baptisms 1813-55 and 1855- ; marriages 1800-44 and 1858-

South Hykeham

- South Hykeham Parish Registers
  www.wparkinson.com/Hykeham/shpage.htm
  Various transcripts and indexes, 19-20th c.

Tetney

- Tetney Transcriptions
  www.wparkinson.com/Tetney.htm
  Baptisms 1813-49; Marriages 1813-37

Norfolk

Civil Registration

- Registration Districts in Norfolk
  www.fhsc.org.uk/genuki/reg/nfk.htm
  Between 1837 and 1930

- Register Offices in Norfolk
  www.norfolk.gov.uk/council/departments/registration/register.htm
  Notes on each office

- [St.Catherine's House Marriage Index, Jan-March, 1849. District 13. Norfolk/North Suffolk
  www.cs.ncl.ac.uk/genuki/StCathsTranscriptions/CATH4913.TXT

Parish & Non-Parochial Registers: Introductory Pages & Lists

- Norfolk Church Records
  www.uea.ac.uk/~s090/genuki/NFK/norfolk/church/
  Genuki introduction

- N.R.O. Parish Registers
  www.norfolk.gov.uk/council/departments/nro/nropratintro.htm
  List of originals and transcripts at Norfolk Record Office

- Norfolk F.H.S. Parish Register Transcripts at Kirby Hall
  www.norfolkfhs.org.uk/church/parishbmd.html
  List of transcripts available for look-up.

- Norfolk
  www.sog.org.uk/prc/norfolk.html
  Parish registers, printed, typescript, *etc.,* in the library of the Society of Genealogists

- Quaker Family History Society: Norfolk
  www.rootsweb.com/~engqfhs/Research/counties/norfolk.htm
  Notes on Quaker records

- Births in Norfolk
  www.rootsweb.com/~engnfk/nfkbrth1.html
  List of entries from submitters

- Brides in Norfolk, England
  www.rootsweb.com/~engnfk/nrfmrsb1.html
  List of entries from submitters

- Grooms in Norfolk, England
  www.rootsweb.com/~engnfk/nrfmrsg1.html
  List of entries from submitters

Indexes

- Parishes covered by Boyd's Marriage Index: Norfolk
  www.englishorigins.com/bmi-parishstats.asp?county=Norfolk

- IGI Batch Numbers: Norfolk Batch Numbers
  freepages.genealogy.rootsweb.com/~tyeroots/norfolk.html

- IGI Batch Numbers for Norfolk, England
  freepages.genealogy.rootsweb.com/~hughwallis/IGIBatchNumbers/
  CountyNorfolk.htm

Newspaper Indexes

- Extracts from *Lynn Advertiser's* Marriages and Deaths 1881-1900
  ourworld.compuserve.com/homepages/Martin__Edwards__2/lynnadv.html

Transcript Collections on the Web

- Norfolk Transcription Archive
  www.genealogy.doun.org/transcriptions/
  Collection of transcripts, listed separately below

Publications

See also Suffolk

- Norfolk F.H.S. Publications: List and Order Form
  www.norfolkfhs.org.uk/sales/
  Includes parish and non-conformist registers

- Mid-Norfolk F.H.S. Publications List
  www.uea.ac.uk/~s300/genuki/NFK/organisations/midnfhs/publications/
  Includes parish register transcriptions, burial indexes and monumental inscriptions, *etc.*

- Norfolk: Church Records: Phillimore's Marriage Registers
  www.uea.ac.uk/~s090/genuki/NFK/norfolk/church/phillimore.shtml
  List of parishes covered, with details of a CD-Rom

Ashmanhaugh

- Norfolk: Tunstead & Happing District: Ashmanhaugh: Baptisms (Parish Register)
  www.genealogy.doun.org/transcriptions.documents.php3?register _id=16&district_id=22&document_type=150
  Covers 1561-1812, with gaps

Barton Turf

- Norfolk: Tunstead & Happing District: Barton Turf: Baptisms (Parish Register)
  www.genealogy.doun.org/transcriptions/documents.php3?register _id=40&district_id=22&document_type=150
  Covers 1840-1900

- Norfolk: Barton Turf: Barton Turf Parish Registers: Surnames of People who come from other Parishes
  www.uea.ac.uk/~s090/genuki/NFK/places/b/barton_turf/pr_strays.shtml

Buxton

- Norfolk: Aylsham District: Buxton: Baptisms (Parish Register)
  www.genealogy.doun.org/transcriptions/documents.php3?register _id=3&district_id=1&document_type=150
  Covers 1718-1896

- Longevity and Child Mortality in Buxton
  www.genealogy.doun.ac.uk/genuki/Transcriptions/articles/view_article.php3?document_id=28918
  Based on the parish register

Cranworth

- Norfolk: Cranworth with Letton: Cranworth with Letton: List of Surnames in the Cranworth with Letton Baptism registers 1652-1855
  www.uea.ac.uk/~s090/genuki/NFK/places/c/cranworth/pr_bapt_names.shtml

- Norfolk: Cranworth with Letton: Cranworth with Letton Parish Registers: list of surnames of People who come from other parishes
  www.uea.ac.uk/~s090/genuki/NFK/places/c/cranworth/pr_strays.shtml

Dunton cum Doughton

- Norfolk: Dunton cum Doughton: Dunton cum Doughton Parish Registers: Surnames of People who come from other Parishes
  www.uea.ac.uk/~s090/genuki/NFK/places/d/dunton_cum_doughton/pr_strays.shtml
  Covers 1785-1835

East Barsham

- Norfolk: East Barsham: East Barsham Parish Registers: People who come from other parishes
  www.uea.ac.uk/~s090/genuki/NFK/places/b/barsham_east/pr_strays.shtml
  Covers 1658-1835

East Tuddenham

- Norfolk: Mitford & Launditch District: East Tuddenham: Baptisms (Bishops Transcripts)
  www.genealogy.doun.org/transcriptions/documents.php3?register _id=663&district_id=16&document_type=160
  Covers 1725-1812, with gaps

Emneth

- Emneth Baptisms Register: Extract from 1808
  freepages.genealogy.rootsweb.com/~cawthorn/Transcripts/Emneth_Baptisms_1808.html

Great Yarmouth

- The Naval Hospital Burials at Yarmouth
  www.genealogy.doun.org/transcriptions/articles/view_article.php3?document_id=25610
  Article partly based on the parish registers

Hoveton

- Norfolk: Tunstead & Happing District: Hoveton St. John: Baptisms (Parish Register)
  www.genealogy.doun.org/transcriptions/documents.php3?register _id=315&district_id=22&documents_type=150
  Covers 1673-1735 & 1766-1899

Islington

See Tilney

Ketteringham

- Norfolk: Henstead District: Ketteringham: Baptisms (Parish Register)
  www.genealogy.doun.org/transcriptions/documents.php3?register __id=
  333&district__id=12&document__type=130
  Covers 1800-1905

Letton

See Cranworth

Morningthorpe

- Norfolk: Depwade District: Morningthorpe: Banns (Parish Register)
  www.genealogy.doun.org/transcriptions/documents.php3?register __id=
  393&district__id=4&document__type=200
  For 1755, 1760, 1766, 1779 & 1781-2

North Tuddenham

- Norfolk: Mitford & Launditch District: North and West Tuddenham:
  Baptisms (Bishop's Transcripts)
  www.genealogy.doun.org/transcriptions/documents.php3?register __id=
  664&district__id=16&document__type=160
  Covers 1725-1811, with gaps

Norwich

- Norfolk: Norwich: Church of England
  www.uea.ac.uk/~s090/genuki/NFK/places/n/norwich/church/
  c__of__e.shtml
  Includes citations to some published registers

Saham Toney

- Norfolk: Saham Toney: Saham Toney Parish Registers: List of Surnames
  of people who come from other Parishes
  www.uea.ac.uk/~s090/genuki/NFK/places/s/saham__toney/
  pr__strays.shtml

Terrington St. Clement

- Terrington St. Clement: Marriages
  genea-logos.bizhosting.com/wisbech/indexes/terrington__st__c.htm
  Index, 1598-9, 1651-5 and 1671-1830

Terrington St. John

- Terrington St. John: Marriages
  www.genea-logos.bizhosting.com/wisbech/indexes/terrington__st__j.htm
  Index, 1706-1812

Thetford

- Norfolk: Thetford District: Thetford St. Mary's: Baptisms
  www.genealogy.doun.org/transcriptions/documents.php3?register __id=
  625&district__id=21&document__type=150
  Covers 1640-1902

- Norfolk: Thetford District: Thetford St. Mary's: Banns
  www.genealogy.doun.org/transcriptions/documents.php3?register __id=
  6258&district__id=21&document__type=200
  Covers 1754-99 and 1825-1902, with gaps

- Norfolk: Thetford District: Thetford St. Mary's: Marriages
  www.genealogy.doun.org/transcriptions/documents.php3?register __id=
  625&district__id=21&document__type=250
  Covers 1653-1902, with gaps

- Norfolk: Thetford District: Thetford St. Mary's: Burials
  www.genealogy.doun.org/transcriptions/documents.php3?register __id=
  625&district__id=21&document__type=300
  Covers 1653-1902, with gaps

- Norfolk: Thetford: Thetford St. Mary's Parish Registers: List of People
  who come from other parishes
  www.uea.ac.uk/~s090/NFK/places/t/thetford/mary/pr__strays.shtml

Tibenham

- Norfolk: Tibenham: Tibenham Parish Registers: List of Surnames of
  people who come from other parishes
  www.uea.ac.uk/~s090/genuki/NFK/places/t/tibenham/pr__strays.shtml

- Norfolk: Tibenham: List of Surnames in the Tibenham Baptism
  Registers 1813-1858
  www.uea.ac.uk/≈s090/genuki/NFK/places/t/tibenham/
  pr__bapt__names.shtml

Tilney

- Tilney cum Islington: Marriages
  genea-logos.bizhosting.com/wisbech/indexes/tilney__Islington.htm
  Index, 1668-1812

Tilney All Saints
- Tilney All Saints: Marriages
  genea-log.bizhosting.com/wisbech/indexes/tilney__all__saints.htm
  Index, 1706-1812

Tilney St. Lawrence
- Tilney St. Lawrence: Marriages
  genea-logos.bizhosting.com/wisbech/indexes/tilney__st__law.htm
  Index, 1707-27 and 1750-1812

Trunch
- Trunch Family History Pages
  www.trunchnorfolk.cwc.net/family.htm
  Includes baptisms 1725-50 & 1800-1912, marriages 1725-1799, and burials 1725-1750, *etc.*

Walsoken
- Walsoken: Marriages
  genea-logos.bizhosting.com/wisbech/indexes/walsoken.htm
  Index, 1668-1812

West Tuddenham
See North Tuddenham

Westfield
- Norfolk: Mitford & Launditch District: Westfield: Baptisms (Bishop's Transcripts)
  www.genealogy.doun.org/transcriptions/documents.php3?register__id= 701&district__id=16&document__type=160
  Covers 1725-1812, with gaps

Westwick
- Norfolk: Tunstead & Happing District: Westwick: Baptisms (Parish Register)
  www.genealogy.doun.org/transcriptions/documents.php3?register __id= 703&district__id=22&document__type=150
  Covers 1790-1812

Whinburgh
- Norfolk: Mitford & Launditch District: Whinburgh: Baptisms (Bishop's Transcripts)
  www.genealogy.doun.org/transcriptions/documents.php3?register __id= 706&district__id=16&document__type=160
  Covers 1725-1811, with gaps

Wiggenhall
- Wiggenhall St. Mary Magdalen: Marriages
  genea-logos.bizhosting.com/wisbech/indexes/wiggenhall__m__m.htm
  Index, 1744-1805

- Wiggenhall St. Peter: Marriages
  genea-logos.bizhosting.com/wisbech/indexes/wiggenhall__p.htm
  Index, 1744-1805

Winfarthing
- Norfolk: Winfarthing: Winfarthing Parish Registers: People who come from other parishes
  www.uea.ac.uk/~s090/genuki/NFK/places/w/winfarthing/ pr__strays.shtml

Northamptonshire

Civil Registration
- Registration Districts in Northamptonshire
  www.fhsc.org.uk/genuki/reg/nth.htm
  Between 1837 and 1930

Parish & Non-Parochial Registers: Introductory Pages & Lists
- Northamptonshire
  www.sog.org.uk/prc/northampton.html
  Parish registers, printed, typescript, *etc.,* in the library of the Society of Genealogists

- Quaker Family History Society: Northamptonshire
  www.rootsweb.com/~engqfhs/Research/counties/northants.htm
  Notes on Quaker records

Indexes
- IGI Batch Numbers: Northamptonshire Batch Numbers
  freepages.genealogy.rootsweb.com/~tyeroots/northamp.html

- IGI Batch Numbers for Northampton, England
  freepages.genealogy.rootsweb.com/~hughwallis/IGIBatchNumbers/ CountyNorthampton.htm

Miscellaneous
- Other Northants & Hunts Parish Register Extracts
  freepages.genealogy.rootsweb.com/~maureenbryon/id82.htm
  Brief extracts from many registers

Benefield
- Benefield Parish Register Extracts
  freepages.genealogy.rootsweb.com/~maureenbryson/id47
  Selected surnames only

Great Gidding
- Great Gidding Parish Register Extracts
  freepages.genealogy.rootsweb.com/~maureenbryson/id58.htm
  Selected surnames only

Gretton
- Gretton Parish Register Extracts
  freepages.genealogy.rootsweb.com/~maureenbryson/id59.htm
  Selected surnames only

- Gretton Parish Records
  www.maurice.skynet.co.uk/genuki/big/eng/NTH/jordan.htm
  Lookups offered

Kings Cliffe
- Kings Cliffe Parish Register Extracts
  freepages.genealogy.rootsweb.com/~maureenbryson/id60.htm
  Selected surnames only

Kingsthorpe
- Kingsthorpe Church Records
  www.maurice.skynet.co.uk/genuki/big/eng/NTH/Kingsthorpe/
  Lookups offered

Oundle
- Oundle Baptisms 1813-1818
  uk-transcriptions.accessgenealogy.com/OundleBapts.htm

- Oundle Baptisms 1813
  uk-transcriptions.accessgenealogy.com/Oundle1813.htm
  Continued at **/Oundle1814.htm** *etc.,* for 1814-1818

- Oundle Parish Register Extracts
  freepages.genealogy.rootsweb.com/~maureenbryson/id49.htm
  Selected surnames only

Thrapston
- Thrapston Parish Register Extracts
  freepages.genealogy.rootsweb.com/~maureenbryson/id78.htm
  Selected surnames only

Northumberland

See also Durham

Civil Registration

- Registration Districts in Northumberland
  www.fhsc.org.uk/genuki/reg/nbl.htm
  Between 1837 and 1930

- Northumberland: Civil Registration
  www.swinhope.demon.co.uk/genuki/NBL/CivilRegistration.html
  Links to addresses of each registration office

- Newcastle Register Office Indexes
  www.ndfhs.org.uk/RegIndex.html
  Important database in progress

- Records held at Newcastle Register Office, Civic Centre
  www.ndfhs.org.uk/RegIndex.html

- [St. Catherine's House Marriage Index, Jan-March, 1849. District 25. Northumberland/Westmoreland]
  www.cs.ncl.ac.uk/genuki/StCathsTranscriptions/CATH4925.TXT

- Cumbrian Genealogy: The St. Catherine's Marriage Index for March Quarter 1849
  sylviamyers.members.beeb.net/StCatsMarchQr1849Marriages.html
  For Northumberland and Westmoreland

Parish & Non-Parochial Registers: Introductory Pages & Lists

- Northumberland Archive Service. Diocese of Newcastle: Anglican Parish Registers
  www.swinhope.demon.co.uk/NROParishRecords.html
  List

- Northumberland Archive Service Methodist Registers
  www.demon.co.uk/NRO/MethRecords.html

- Northumberland Archive Service. Presbyterian and Congregational Registers
  www.swinhope.demon.co.uk/NRO/UReform.html

- Northumberland Archive Service. Roman Catholic Registers
  www.swinhope.demon.co.uk/NRO/Catholic.html

- Northumberland Archive Service. Civil Cemetery Records
  www.swinhope.demon.co.uk/NRO/Cemeteries.html

- Newcastle upon Tyne City Libraries & Arts. Local Studies Library. Genealogy guide no. 5. Parish Register Transcripts and Indexes
  www.swinhope.demon.co.uk/genuki/NBL/NCLLIB/NCLGG5.html

- Northumberland Archive Service: Transcripts in Berwick upon Tweed Record Office.
  www.swinhope.demon.co.uk/NRO/Berwick.html
  Of parish registers, monumental inscriptions, *etc.*

- Northumberland Archive Service. Registers of other Denominations.
  www.swinhope.demon.co.uk/NRO/OtherDenoms.htm

- Durham County Record Office. Handlist 7. Northumberland and North Yorkshire Transcripts and Indexes (Church of England)
  www.durham.gov.uk/durhamcc/usp.nsf/lookup/pdfhandlists/
                                      $file/handlist07.pdf

- Northumberland Parish Registers
  www.ndfhs.org.uk/Library/index.html
  Click on title. In the Library of the Northumberland & Durham Family History Society

- Northumberland & Durham Family History Society: Transcripts on Computer at Bolbec Hall. Part 2. Northumberland
  www.ndfhs.org.uk
  Click on title. Parish registers

- Northumberland
  www.sog.org.uk/prc/northumberland.html
  Parish registers, printed, typescript, *etc.,* in the library of the Society of Genealogists

- Quaker Family History Society: Northumberland
  www.rootsweb.com/~engqfhs/Research/counties/nortum.htm
  Notes on Quaker records

Indexes

- Free Reg: Northumberland
  freereg.rootsweb.com/parishes/nbl/index.htm
  Details of the registers currently included in a project to index births, deaths and marriages

- Parishes covered by Boyd's Marriage Index: Northumberland
  www.englishorigins.com/bmi-parishstats.asp?county=Northumberland

- IGI Batch Numbers: Northumberland Batch Numbers
  freepages.genealogy.rootsweb.com/~tyeroots/north.html

- IGI Batch Numbers for Northumberland, England
  freepages.genealogy.rootsweb.com/~hughwallis/IGIBatchNumbers/
  CountyNorthumberland.htm

Publications

- Northumberland & Durham Family History Society Publications on Microfiche
  www.ndfhs.org.uk/Fiche.html
  Includes parish registers, monumental inscriptions, *etc.*

- Northfiche: Northumberland Parish Register Transcripts & Indexes
  www.jwillans.freeserve.co.uk/northficnbl.html
  Fiche for sale

- Northumberland Record Office: Microfiche for Sale
  www.swinhope.demon.co.uk/NRO/Fiche.html

Allendale

- Allendale Church Records
  www.swinhope.demon.co.uk/genuki/NBL/Allendale/ChurchRecords.html
  List with locations

Alnwick

- Alnwick: Church Records
  www.swinhope.demon.co.uk/genuki/NBL/Alnwick/ChurchRecords.html
  List with locations

Ancroft

- Ancroft: Church Records
  www.swinhope.demon.co.uk/genuki/NBL/Ancroft/ChurchRecords.html
  List with locations

Bamburgh

- Bamburgh: Church Records
  www.swinhope.demon.co.uk/genuki/NBL/Bamburgh/ChurchRecords.html
  List with locations

Bedlington

- Bedlington: Church Records
  www.swinhope.demon.co.uk/genuki/NBL/Bedlington/ChurchRecords. html
  List with locations

- Marriages from the Registers of Bedlington (1813-1837)
  www.cs.ncl.ac.uk/genuki/Transcriptions/NBL/MBED.html

Belford

- Belford: Church Records
  www.swinhope.demon.co.uk/genuki/NBL/Belford/ChurchRecords.html
  List with locations

- Belford Baptisms 1813-11837
  www.cs.ncl.ac.uk/genuki/Transcriptions/NBL/XBFD.html

Bellingham

- Bellingham: Church Records
  www.swinhope.demon.co.uk/genuki/NBL/Bellingham/ChurchRecords.html

Berwick

- Berwick: Church Records
  www.swinhope.demon.co.uk/genuki/NBL/Berwick/ChurchRecords.html
  List with locations

Blanchland

- Blanchland: Church Records
  www.swinhope.demon.co.uk/genuki/NBL/Blanchland/ChurchRecords.html
  List with locations

- Marriages from the Blanchland Registers (1753-1837)
  www.cs.ncl.ac.uk/genuki/Transcriptions/NBL/BLA.html

Bothal

- Bothal: Church Records
  www.swinhope.demon.co.uk/genuki/NBL/BothallChurchRecords.html
  List with locations

- Marriages from the Registers of Bothal (1813-1837)
  www.cs.ncl.ac.uk/genuki/Transcriptions/NBL/MBOT.html

Bywell

- Bywell St. Andrew: Church Records
  www.swinhope.demon.co.uk/genuki/NBL/BywellStAndrew/
  ChurchRecords.html

  List with locations

- Marriages from the Bywell St Andrew Registers (1686-1837)
  www.cs.ncl.ac.uk/genuki/Transcriptions/NBL/BSA.html

- Marriages from the Bywell St Peter Registers (1663-1837)
  www.cs.ncl.ac.uk/genuki/Transcriptions/NBL/BSP.html

Carham

- Carham: Church Records
  www.swinhope.demon.co.uk/genuki/NBL/Carham/ChurchRecords.html
  List with locations

Carrshield

- Baptisms from the Registers of Carrshield (1823-1837)
  www.cs.ncl.ac.uk/genuki/Transcriptions/NBL/XCSH.html
  In Allendale parish

Chatton

- Chatton: Church Records
  www.swinhope.demon.co.uk/genuki/NBL/Chatton/ChurchRecords.html
  List with locations

Chollerton

- Chollerton: Church Records
  www.swinhope.demon.co.uk/genuki/NBL/Chollerton/ChurchRecords. html
  List with locations

Corbridge

- Corbridge: Church Records
  www.swinhope.demon.co.uk/genuki/NBL/Corbridge/ChurchRecords.html
  List with locations

Corsenside

- Corsenside: Church Records
  www.swinhope.demon.co.uk/genuki/NBL/Corsenside/ChurchRecords.html
  List with locations

Cramlington

- Cramlington: Church Records
  www.swinhope.demon.co.uk/genuki/NBL/Cramlington/ChurchRecords.html
  List with locations

- Marriages from the Registers of Cramlington (1814-1836)
  www.cs.ncl.ac.uk/genuki/Transcriptions/NBL/MCRA.html

Dinnington

- Dinnington: Church Records
  www.swinhope.demon.co.uk/genuki/NBL/Dinnington/ChurchRecords. html

Earsdon

- Earsdon: Church Records
  www.swinhope.demon.co.uk/genuki/NBL/Earsdon/ChurchRecords.html
  List with locations

- Selected Entries from Earsdon Registers 1626-1750
  www.swinhope.demon.co.uk/genuki/NBL/Earsdon/EarsReg.html
  From Craster's *History of Northumberland,* originally published 1909

- Marriages from the Registers of Earsdon (1813-1837)
  www.cs.ncl.ac.uk/genuki/Transcriptions/NBL/MEAR.html

Edlingham

- Edlingham: Church Records
  www.swinhope.demon.co.uk/genuki/NBL/Edlingham/ChurchRecords.html
  List with locations

Eglingham

- Eglingham: Church Records
  www.swinhope.demon.co.uk/genuki/NBL/Eglingham/ChurchRecords.html
  List with locations

Ellingham

- Ellingham: Church Records
  www.swinhope.demon.co.uk/genuki/NBL/ellingham/ChurchRecords.html

Elsdon

- Elsdon: Church Records
  www.swinhope.demon.co.uk/genuki/NBL/Elsdon/ChurchRecords.html
  List with locations

Falstone
- Falstone: Church Records
  www.swinhope.demon.co.uk/genuki/NBL/Falstone/ChurchRecords.html
  List with locations

Felton
- Felton: Church Records
  www.swinhope.demon.co.uk/genuki/NBL/Felton/ChurchRecords.html
  List with locations

Ford
- Ford: Church Records
  www.swinhope.demon.co.uk/genuki/NBL/Ford/ChurchRecords.html
  List with locations

Gosforth
- Gosforth: Church Records
  www.swinhope.demon.co.uk/genuki/NBL/Gosforth/ChurchRecords.html
  List with locations

- Marriages from the Registers of Gosforth (1813-1837)
  www.cs.ncl.ac.uk/genuki/Transcriptions/NBL/MGOS.html

Halton
- Halton: Church Records
  www.swinhope.demon.co.uk/genuki/NBL/Halton/ChurchRecords.html
  List with locations

- Baptisms from the Registers of Halton (1813-1837)
  www.cs.ncl.ac.uk/genuki/Transcriptions/NBL/XHAL.html

- Marriages from the Halton Registers (1654-1769)
  www.cs.ncl.ac.uk/genuki/Transcriptions/NBL/HAL.html

Haltwhistle
- Haltwhistle: Church Records
  www.swinhope.demon.co.uk/genuki/NBL/Haltwhistle/ChurchRecords.html
  List with locations

Hartburn
- Hartburn: Church Records
  www.swinhope.demon.co.uk/genuki/NBL/Hartburn/ChurchRecords.html
  List with locations

Haydon Bridge
- Haydon Bridge: Church Records
  www.swinhope.demon.co.uk/genuki/NBL/HaydonBridge/
                                   ChurchRecords.html

  List with locations

- Marriages from the Registers of Haydon Bridge (1813-1837)
  www.cs.ncl.ac.uk/genuki/Transcriptions/NBL/MHBR.html

Hebburn
- Hebburn: Church Records
  www.swinhope.demon.co.uk/genuki/NBL/Hebburn/ChurchRecords.html
  List with locations

- Marriages from the Registers of Hebburn (1813-1836)
  www.cs.ncl.ac.uk/genuki/Transcriptions/NBL/MHEB.html

Heddon on the Wall
- Heddon: Church Records
  www.swinhope.demon.co.uk/genuki/NBL/Heddon/ChurchRecords.html
  List with locations

Hexham
- Hexham: Church Records
  www.swinhope.demon.co.uk/genuki/NBL/Hexham/ChurchRecords.html
  List with locations

- Marriages from the Hexham Registers (1540-1599)
  www.cs.ncl.ac.uk/Transcriptions/NBL/HEX1540.htm
  Continued to 1699 at /HEX1600.html

- Marriages from the Hexham Registers (1540-1599)
  www.cs.ncl.ac.uk/genuki/Transcriptions/NBL/HEX1540.html
  Continued as follows:
  1600-1699 /HEX1600.html
  1700-1749 /HEX1700.html
  1750-1799 /HEX1750.html
  1800-1837 /HEX1800.html

Holy Island
- Holy Island: Church Records
  www.swinhope.demon.co.uk/genuki/NBL/HolyIsland/ChurchRecords. html
  List with locations

- Baptisms from the Registers of Holy Island (1813-1837)
  www.cs.ncl.ac.uk/genuki/Transcriptions/NBL/XHIS.html

- Burials from the Holy Island Registers (1813-1837)
  www.cs.ncl.ac.uk/genuki/Transcriptions/NBL/BHIS.html

Horton
- Horton: Church Records
  www.swinhope.demon.co.uk/genuki/NBL/Horton/ChurchRecords.html

- Marriages from the Horton Registers (1665-1837)
  www.cs.ncl.ac.uk/genuki/Transcriptions/NBL/HOR.html

Kirkhaugh
- Marriages from the Kirkhaugh Registers (1761-1837)
  www.cs.ncl.ac.uk/genuki/Transcriptions/NBL/KHG.html

Kirkheaton
- Kirkheaton: Church Records
  www.swinhope.demon.co.uk/genuki/NBL/Kirkheaton/ChurchRecords.html
  List with locations

Kirknewton
- Kirknewton: Church Records
  www.swinhope.demon.co.uk/genuki/NBL/Kirknewton/ChurchRecords.html
  List with locations

Kirkwhelpington
- Kirkwhelpington: Church Records
  www.swinhope.demon.co.uk/genuki/NBL/Kirkwhelpington/ChurchRecords.html

  List with locations

Knaresdale
- Knaresdale: Church Records
  www.swinhope.demon.co.uk/genuki/NBL/Knaresdale/ChurchRecords.html
  List with locations

- Marriages from the Knaresdale Registers (1701-1837)
  www.cs.ncl.ac.uk/genuki/Transcriptions/NBL/KND.html

Lambley
- Marriages from the Lambley Registers (1743-1836)
  www.cs.ncl.ac.uk/genuki/Transcriptions/NBL/LBY.html

Lesbury
- Lesbury: Church Records
  www.swinhope.demon.co.uk/genuki/NBL/Lesbury/ChurchRecords.html
  List with locations

Longbenton
- Longbenton: Church Records
  www.swinhope.demon.co.uk/genuki/NBL/Longbenton/ChurchRecords. html
  List with locations

- Baptisms from the Registers of Longbenton (1813-1821)
  www.cs.ncl.ac.uk/genuki/Transcriptions/NBL/XLBN1813.html
  Continued for 1822-1829 at **/XLBN1822.html**
  and for 1830-1837 at **/XLBN1830.html**

- Marriages from the Longbenton Registers (1653-1799)
  www.cs.ncl.ac.uk/genuki/Transcriptions/NBL/LBN1653.html
  Continued to 1837 at **/LBN1800.html**

- Longbenton 1653-1837
  homepages.rootsweb.com/~mwi/mlongben.txt
  Marriages

- Burials from the Longbenton Registers (1813-1826)
  www.cs.ncl.ac.uk/genuki/Transcriptions/NBL/BLBN1813.html

- Burials from the Longbenton Registers (1827-1837)
  www.cs.ncl.ac.uk/genuki/Transcriptions/NBL/BLBN1827.html

Longframlington
- Longframlington: Church Records
  www.swinhope.demon.co.uk/genuki/NBL/Longframlington/ChurchRecords.html

  List with locations

Longhorsley
- Longhorsley: Church Records
  www.swinhope.demon.co.uk/genuki/NBL/Longhorsley/ChurchRecords.html
  List with locations

Lucker
- Lucker: Church Records
  www.swinhope.demon.co.uk/genuki/NBL/Lucker/ChurchRecords.html
  List with locations

Matfen
- Matfen Marriages, 1846-1901
  www.cs.ncl.ac.uk/genuki/Transcriptions/NBL/Matfen.html
  In Stamfordham parish

Mitford
- Mitford: Church Records
  www.swinhope.demon.co.uk/genuki/NBL/Mitford/ChurchRecords.html
  List with locations

- Marriages from the Registers of Mitford (1813-1836)
  www.cs.ncl.ac.uk/genuki/Transcriptions/NBL/MMIT.html

Morpeth
- Morpeth: Church Records
  www.swinhope.demon.co.uk/genuki/NBL/Morpeth/ChurchRecords.html
  List with locations

- Marriages from the Registers of Morpeth (1813-1837)
  www.cs.ncl.ac.uk/genuki/Transcriptions/NBL/MMOR.html

Netherwitton
- Netherwitton: Church Records
  www.swinhope.demon.co.uk/genuki/NBL/Netherwitton/
  ChurchRecords.html

  List with locations

- Some Netherwitton Baptisms 1805-6
  www.jwillans.freeserve.co.uk/sample.html
  Facsimile of original register

Newbiggin
- Newbiggin: Church Records
  www.swinhope.demon.co.uk/genuki/NBL/Newbiggin/ChurchRecords.html
  List with locations

Newbrough
- Newbrough: Church Records
  www.swinhope.demon.co.uk/genuki/NBL/Newbrough/ChurchRecords.html
  List with locations

Newburn
- Newburn: Church Records
  www.swinhope.demon.co.uk/genuki/NBL/Newburn/ChurchRecords.html
  List with locations

- Marriages from the Newburn Registers (1659-1799)
  www.cs.ncl.ac.uk/genuki/Transcriptions/NBL/NBN1659.html
  Continued to 1837 at /NBN1800.html

Newcastle Upon Tyne
- Marriages from the Newcastle Courant 1841
  www.cs.ncl.ac.uk/genuki/Transcriptions/NBL/MCOUR1841.html

- Newcastle-upon-Tyne: Records of Non-Conformist Churches and
  Congregations
  www.swinhope.demon.co.uk/genuki/NBL/Newcastle/nonconf.html

- Burials at Newcastle General Cemetery, 1836-1837
  www.cs.ncl.ac.uk/genuki/Transcriptions/NBL/BNGC.html
  Register

- Newcastle All Saints: Church Records
  www.swinhope.demon.co.uk/genuki/NBL/Newcastle/AllSaints/
  ChurchRecords.html

  List with locations

- Newcastle, St. Andrew: Church Records
  www.swinhope.demon.co.uk/genuki/NBL/Newcastle/StAndrews/
  ChurchRecords.html

  List with locations

- Marriages from the Newcastle St Andrew Registers (1589-1599)
  www.cs.ncl.ac.uk/genuki/Transcriptions/NBL/NSA1589.html
  Continued as follows:
  ```
  1600-1649  /NSA1600.html
  1650-1699  /NSA1650.html
  1700-1749  /NSA1700.html
  1750-1799  /NSA1750.html
  1800-1824  /NSA1800.html
  1825-1837  /NSA1825.html
  ```

- Baptisms from the Registers of Newcastle, St Ann (1813-1835)
  www.cs.ncl.ac.uk/genuki/Transcriptions/NBL/XNAN.html
- Burials from the Registers of Newcastle, St Ann (1828-1837)
  www.cs.ncl.ac.uk/genuki/Transcriptions/NBL/BNAN.html
- Newcastle, St John: Church Records
  www.swinhope.demon.co.uk/genuki/NBL/Newcastle/StJohns/
  ChurchRecords.html

  List with locations

- Marriages from the Registers of St John (1813-1823)
  www.cs.ncl.ac.uk/genuki/Transcriptions/NBL/MNSJ1813.html
  In Newcastle. Continued as follows:
    1824-1828 MNSJ1824.html
    1829-1833 MNSJ1829.html
    1834-1837 MNSJ1834.html
- Newcastle St. Nicholas: Church Records
  www.swinhope.demon.co.uk/genuki/NBL/Newcastle/StNicholas/
  ChurchRecords.html

  List with locations

- Marriages from the Registers of St Nicholas (1813-1837)
  www.cs.ncl.ac.uk/genuki/Transcriptions/NBL/MNSN.html
  In Newcastle

Norham
- Norham: Church Records
  www.swinhope.demon.co.uk/genuki/NBL/Norham/ChurchRecords.html
  List with locations

North Shields
- Deaths and Fatal Injuries at North Shields on May 3rd 1941
  www.swinhope.demon.co.uk/genuki/NBL/Tynemouth/Shelter.html
  Air-raid deaths

Ovingham
- Ovingham: Church Records
  www.swinhope.demon.co.uk/genuki/NBL/Ovingham/ChurchRecords.html
  List with locations

- Baptisms from the Registers of Ovingham (1813-1837)
  www.cs.ncl.ac.uk/genuki/Transcriptions/NBL/XOVI.html

- Marriages from the Ovingham Registers (1679-1769)
  www.cs.ncl.ac.uk/genuki/Transcriptions/NBL/OVI.html
  Continued to 1837 at /OVI1770.html
- Burials from the registers of Ovingham (1813-1837)
  www.cs.ncl.ac.uk/genuki/Transcriptions/NBL/BOVI.html

Ponteland
- Ponteland: Church Records
  www.swinhope.demon.co.uk/genuki/NBLPonteland/ChurchRecords.html
  List with locations

- Marriages from the Registers of Ponteland (1813-1837)
  www.cs.ncl.ac.uk/genuki/Transcriptions/NBL/MPON.html

Rennington
- Rennington: Church Records
  www.swinhope.demon.co.uk/genuki/NBL/Rennington/
  ChurchRecords.html

  List with locations

- Burials from the Registers of Rennington (1813-1837)
  www.cs.ncl.ac.uk/genuki/Transcriptions/NBL/BREN.html

Rock
- Rock: Church Records
  www.swinhope.demon.co.uk/genuki/NBL/Rock/ChurchRecords.html
  List with locations

- Baptisms from the Registers of Rock (1813-1837)
  www.cs.ncl.ac.uk/genuki/Transcriptions/NBL/XROC.html

- Burials from the Registers of Rock (1813-1837)
  www.cs.ncl.ac.uk/genuki/Transcriptions/NBL/BROC.html

Rothbury
- Rothbury: Church Records
  www.swinhope.demon.co.uk/genuki/NBL/Rothbury/ChurchRecords.html
  List with locations

Shotley
- Shotley: Church Records
  www.swinhope.demon.co.uk/genuki/NBL/Shotley/ChurchRecords.html
  List with locations

- Marriages from the Shotley Registers (1670-1837)
  www.cs.ncl.ac.uk/genuki/Transcriptions/NBL/SHL.html

Simonburn
- Simonburn: Church Records
  www.swinhope.demon.co.uk/genuki/NBL/Simonburn/ChurchRecords.html
  List with locations

Slaley
- Slaley: Church Records
  www.swinhope.demon.co.uk/genuki/NBL/Slaley/ChurchRecords.html
  List with locations

- Marriages from the Slaley Registers (1725-1837)
  www.cs.ncl.ac.uk/genuki/Transcriptions/NBL/SLA.html

Stamfordham
See Matfen

Thorneyburn
- Thorneyburn: Church Records
  www.swinhope.demon.co.uk/genuki/NBL/Thorneyburn/
  ChurchRecords.html

  List with locations

Tweedmouth
- Tweedmouth: Church Records
  www.swinhope.demon.co.uk/genuki/NBL/Tweedmouth/
  ChurchRecords.html

  List with locations

Tynemouth
- Tynemouth: Church Records
  www.swinhope.demon.co.uk/genuki/NBL/Tynemouth/ChurchRecords.html
  List with locations

- Tynemouth Parish: Records of Non-Conformist Churches and
  Congregations
  www.swinhope.demon.co.uk/genuki/NBL/Tynemouth/tynnconf.html
  List with locations

- Marriages from the Registers of Tynemouth (1607-1679)
  www.cs.ncl.ac.uk/genuki/Transcriptions/NBL/MTYN1607.html
  Continued as follows:
  1680-1719 /MTYN1680.html   1720-1754 /MTYN1720.html
  1813-1821 /MTYN1813.html   1822-1829 /MTYN1822.html
  1830-1837 /MTYN1830.html

- Tynemouth Society of Friends: Burials 1661-1818
  www.cs.ncl.ac.uk/genuki/Transcriptions/NBL/BTYN-SoF.html

Ulgham
- Marriages from the Registers of Ulgham (1755-1834)
  www.cs.ncl.ac.uk/genuki/Transcriptions/NBL/MULG.html

Wallsend
- Wallsend: Church Records
  www.swinhope.demon.co.uk/genuki/NBL/Wallsend/ChurchRecords.html
  List with locations

- Marriages from the Registers of Wallsend (1813-1837)
  www.cs.ncl.ac.uk/genuki/Transcriptions/NBL/MWAL.html

Warden
- Warden: Church Records
  www.swinhope.demon.co.uk/genuki/NBL/Warden/ChurchRecords.html
  List with locations

- Marriages from the Registers of Warden (1813-1837)
  www.cs.ncl.ac.uk/genuki/Transcriptions/NBL/MWDN.html

- Burials from the Warden Registers (1813-1901)
  www.cs.ncl.ac.uk/genuki/Transcriptions/NBL/BWDN.html

Warkworth
- Warkworth: Church Records
  www.swinhope.demon.co.uk/genuki/NBL/Warkworth/ChurchRecords.html
  List with locations

Whalton
- Whalton: Church Records
  www.swinhope.demon.co.uk/genuki/NBL/Whalton/ChurchRecords.html
  List with locations

Whitfield
- Marriages from the Whitfield Registers (1606-1837)
  www.cs.ncl.ac.uk/genuki/Transcriptions/NBL/WTF.html

Whitley
- Whitley: Church Records
  www.swinhope.demon.co.uk/genuki/NBL/Whitley/ChurchRecords.html
  List with locations

Whittingham
- Whittingham: Church Records
  www.swinhope.demon.co.uk/genuki/NBL/Whittingham/
  ChurchRecords.html

  List with locations

Whittonstall
- Whittonstall: Church Records
  www.swinhope.demon.co.uk/genuki/NBL/Whittonstall/
  ChurchRecords.html

  List with locations

Widdrington
- Widdrington: Church Records
  www.swinhope.demon.co.uk/genuki/NBL/Widdrington/
  ChurchRecords.html

  List with locations

- Marriages from the Registers of Widdrington (1826-1837)
  www.cs.ncl.ac.uk/genuki/Transcriptions/NBL/MWID.html

Woodhorn
- Woodhorn: Church Records
  www.swinhope.demon.co.uk/genuki/NBL/Woodhorn/ChurchRecord.shtml
  List with locations

- Marriages from the Registers of Woodhorn (1813-1839)
  www.cs.ncl.ac.uk/genuki/Transcriptions/NBL/MWOO.html

Wooler
- Wooler: Church Records
  www.swinhope.demon.co.uk/genuki/NBL/Wooler/ChurchRecords.html
  List with locations

Nottinghamshire

Civil Registration
- Registration Districts in Nottinghamshire
  www.fhsc.org.uk/genuki/reg/ntt.htm
  Betwen 1837 and 1930

Parish & Non-Parochial registers: Introductory Pages & Lists
- Nottinghamshire Family History Society: Parish Register List for Searching
  www.nottsfhs.org.uk
  Click on 'Research' and 'Parishes Searched'. List of transcripts held.

- Nottinghamshire
  www.sog.org.uk/prc/nottinghamshire.html
  Parish registers, printed, typescript, *etc.,* in the library of the Society of Genealogists

- Quaker Family History Society: Nottinghamshire
  www.rootsweb.com/~engqfhs/Research/counties/notts.htm
  Notes on Quaker records

Indexes
- IGI Batch Numbers: Nottinghamshire Batch Numbers
  freepages.genealogy.rootsweb.com/~tyeroots/notting.html

- IGI Batch Numbers for Nottingham, England
  freepages.genealogy.rootsweb.com/~hughwallis/IGIBatchNumbers/
  CountyNottingham.htm

Marriage Licences
- Nottinghamshire Marriage Licences
  homepages.nildram.co.uk/~jimella/marlic01.htm
  For 1578-1604

- Nottinghamshire Marriage Licence Bonds
  freespace.virgin.net/guy.etchells/NML.htm
  1701 only available at present, but more in progress

Collections of Transcripts on the Web

- Nottinghamshire Church Register Transcriptions & Indexes
www.neep.demon.co.uk/nottsreg/index.html
List of on-line transcripts, with look-up service for other registers

- Nottinghamshire Stray Marriages
homepages.nildram.co.uk/~jimella/strays01.htm
Collection of web-pages, separately listed below

- Selected Nottinghamshire Parish Registers
homepages.nildram.co.uk/~jimella/preg01.htm
Collection of web-pages, individually listed below, with separate index

- Nottinghamshire Stray Marriages
homepages.nildram.co.uk/~jimella/strays01.htm
Individual places separately listed by place below

Publications

- Nottinghamshire Family History Society: the Online Shop
www.nottsfhs.org.uk/bookshop/system/index.html
Includes parish registers and monumental inscriptions published by the society

Beckingham

- Parish register transcriptions of Beckingham, Nottinghamshire, for the years 1634, 1637 & 1641
homepages.nildram.co.uk/~jimella/beck01.htm

Bilborough

- Bilborough, Nottinghamshire: Marriages 1569-1812
www.neep.demon.co.uk/fhist/notts/bilborough__marr1.html

Bilsthorpe

- Nottinghamshire Stray Marriages in Bilsthorpe
homepages.nildram.co.uk/~jimella/strays09.htm

Bingham

- Bingham Parish Records
freespace.virgin.net/guy.etchells/Bnprindex.htm
Marriages, 1598-1812

Bleasby

- Parish Register Transcripts of Bleasby, Nottinghamshire for the Year 1633
homepages.nildram.co.uk/~jimella/bleas01.htm

Blidworth

- Parish Register Transcripts of Blidworth, Nottinghamshire for the Year 1638
homepages.nildram.co.uk/~jimella/blid01.htm

Calverton

- Parish Register Transcripts of Calverton, Nottinghamshire for the Years 1617 & 1623
homepages.nildram.co.uk/~jimella/calvpr01.htm

- Nottinghamshire Stray Marriages in Calverton
homepages.nildram.co.uk/~jimella/strays04.htm

Cropwell Bishop

- Parish Register Transcripts of Cropwell Bishop, Nottinghamshire for the Years 1638 & 1641
homepages.nildram.co.uk/~jimella/crpbish1.htm

Darlton

- Parish Register Transcripts of Darlton, Nottinghamshire for the Years 1622, 1633 & 1641
homepages.nildram.co.uk/~jimella/darl01.htm

Dunham

- Parish Register Transcripts of Dunham, Nottinghamshire for the Year 1641
homepages.nildram.co.uk/~jimella/dun01.htm

Eakring

- Nottinghamshire Stray Marriages in Eakring
homepages.nildram.co.uk/~jimella/strays30.htm

Edingley

- Parish Register Transcripts of Edingley, Nottinghamshire for the Year 1638
homepages.nildram.co.uk/~jimella/eding01.htm

Elston

- Elston Chapel Marriages (1584-1721)
  freespace.virgin.net/guy.etchells/ECM1.htm
  Continued to 1814 at **/ECM2.htm**

- Elston Village Marriages (1573-1716)
  freespace.virgin.net/guy.etchells/EVM1.htm
  Continued as follows:
    1717-51 **/EVM2.htm**
    1751-1811 **/EVM3.htm**

Elton on the Hill

- Elton-on-the-Hill Parish Records
  freespace.virgin.net/guy.etchells/Eltprindex.htm
  Marriages, 1593-1812

Farnsfield

- Parish Register Transcripts of Farnsfield, Nottinghamshire for the Year 1623
  homepages.nildram.co.uk/~jimella/farnsfd1.htm

Halam

- Parish Register Transcripts of Halam, Nottinghamshire for the Years 1622 & 1637
  homepages.nildram.co.uk/~jimella/halam1.htm

Halloughton

- Parish Register Transcripts of Halloughton, Nottinghamshire for the Years 1622, 1633 & 1641
  homepages.nildram.co.uk/~jimella/hall01.htm

Hickling

- Hickling Parish Records
  freespace.genealogy.rootsweb.com/~framland/par/Hiprindex.htm
  Marriages 1646-1812

Holme

- Parish Register Transcripts of Holme, Nottinghamshire for the Years 1623, 1625, 1628, 1638 & 1641
  homepages.nildram.co.uk/~jimella/holme1.htm

Kirklington

- Parish Register Transcripts of Kirklington, Nottinghamshire for the Years 1622 & 1638
  homepages.nildram.co.uk/~jimella/kirk1.htm

Lambley

- Nottinghamshire Stray Marriages in Lambley
  homepages.nildram.co.uk/~jimella/strays07.htm

Lenton

- Lenton Parish & Priory Records
  freespace.virgin.net/guy.etchells/Lenprindex.htm
  Abstracts of Lenton Register, 1540-1848

Little Carlton

- Little Carlton Transcriptions
  www.wparkinson.com/Little%20Carlton.htm
  Baptisms 1813-1978; marriages 1813-37

Morton

- Parish Register Transcripts of Morton, Nottinghamshire for the Years 1622 & 1623
  homepages.nildram.co.uk/~jimella/morton1.html

Newark

- Church Register Transcriptions, Newark, Nottinghamshire
  www.neep.demon.co.uk/nottsreg/newark/index.html
  Also available at **www.parishregisters.co.uk** (click on 'Nottinghamshire' and 'Newark') Includes St. Leonards baptisms 1873-5, and St. Mary burials 1811-12. Also offers lookups for other Newark registers

North Muskham

- Parish Register Transcripts of North Muskham, Nottinghamshire, for the Years 1623, 1633 & 1638
  homepages.nildram.co.uk/~jimella/nmusk1.htm

Norwell

- Parish Register Transcripts of Norwell, Nottinghamshire for the Years 1638 & 1641
  homepages.nildram.co.uk/~jimella/norwell1.htm

Oxton
- Parish Register Transcripts of Oxton, Nottinghamshire, for the Year 1622
  homepages.nildram.co.uk/~jimella/oxtonpr1.htm

- Nottinghamshire Stray Marriages in Oxton
  homepages.nildram.co.uk/~jimella/strays06.htm

Ragnall
- Parish Register Transcripts of Ragnall, Nottinghamshire, for the Year 1623
  homepages.nildram.co.uk/~jimella/ragnall1.htm

South Muskham
- Parish Register Transcripts of South Muskham, Nottinghamshire for the Year 1623
  homepages.nildram.co.uk/~jimella/smusk1.htm

Southwell
- Parish Register Transcripts of Southwell, Nottinghamshire for the Years 1633 & 1641
  homepages.nildram.co.uk/~jimella/sthwll1.htm

Strelley
- Strelley, Nottinghamshire: Marriages 1665-1812
  www.neep.demon.co.uk/fhist/notts/strelley__marriages1.html

Sutton in Ashfield
- Parliament Street Chapel & Burial Ground: some burials between 1775 & 1797
  www.genealogy-links.co.uk/html/ash.burials.html
  In Sutton in Ashfield

Thurgaton
- Nottinghamshire Stray Marriages in Thurgaton
  homepages.nildram.co.uk/~jimella/strays05.htm

Tythby
- Parish Register Transcripts of Tithby, Nottinghamshire, for the Year 1625
  homepages.nildram.co.uk/~jimella/tithby1.htm

- Nottinghamshire Stray Marriages in Tithby
  homepages.nildram.co.uk/~jimella/strays08.htm

Upton
- Parish Register Transcripts of Upton, Nottinghamshire, for the Years 1633 & 1638
  homepages.nildram.co.uk/~jimella/upton01.htm

Wollaton
- Baptisms at Wollaton St. Leonards 1732-1800
  www.genuki.org.uk/big/eng/Notts/Transcriptions/wollbap1.txt

Woodborough
- Parish Register Transcripts of Woodborough, Nottinghamshire, for the Years 1623, 1627, 1637, 1638 & 1640
  homepages.nildram.co.uk/~jimella/woodbr01.htm

Rutland

Civil Registration
- Registration Districts in Rutland
  www.fhsc.org.uk/genuki/reg/rut.htm
  Between 1837 and 1930

Parish & Non-Parochial Registers: Introductory Pages & Lists
- Rutland
  www.sog.org.uk/prc/rutland.html
  Parish registers, printed, typescript, *etc.,* in the library of the Society of Genealogists

Indexes
- IGI Batch Numbers: Rutland Batch Numbers
  freepages.genealogy.rootsweb.com/~tyeroots/rutland.html

- IGI Batch Numbers for Rutland, England
  freepages.genealogy.rootsweb.com/~hughwallis/IGIBatchNumbers/CountyRutland.htm

North Luffenham
- Marriages at North Luffenham, 1564-1749
  www.uk-genealogy.org.uk/england/Rutland/NorthLuffenham/index.html
  Searchable database

Staffordshire

Civil Registration
- Registration Districts in Staffordshire
  www.fhsc.org.uk/genuki/reg/sts.htm
  Between 1837 and 1930

- Staffordshire Registration Service
  www..staffordshire.gov.uk/registration/

- Registration Service
  www.wolverhampton.gov.uk/wcidaz/registra.htm
  At Wolverhampton

- [St. Catherine's House Marriage Index, Jan-March, 1849. District 17. Staffordshire]
  www.cs.ncl.ac.uk/genuki/StCathsTranscriptions/CATH4917.TXT

Parish & Non-Parochial Registers: Introductory Pages & Lists
See also Warwickshire

- Staffordshire Church Records: Location, Guides & Indexes
  www.genuki.org.uk/big/eng/STS/ChurchRecords.html

- Nonconformist & Roman Catholic Registers
  www.wolverhamptonarchives.dial.pipex.com/non-con.htm
  At Wolverhampton Archives

- Staffordshire
  www.sog.org.uk/prc/staffordshire.html
  Parish registers, printed, typescript, *etc.,* in the library of the Society of Genealogists

- Quaker Family History Society: Staffordshire
  www.rootsweb.com/~engqfhs/Research/counties/staffs.htm
  Notes on Quaker records

Indexes
- B.M.S.G.H. Search Services
  www.bmsgh.org/search/sea1.html
  Details of various marriage and burial indexes *etc.,* for Staffordshire, Warwickshire and Worcestershire

- Free Reg: Staffordshire
  freereg.rootsweb.com/parishes/sts/index.htm
  Details of the registers currently included in a project to index births, marriages and deaths

- Privately Owned Indexes Relating to Staffordshire, Warwickshire or Worcestershire
  www.bmsgh.org/search/sea4.html
  Lists various indexes to parish registers *etc.*

- Staffordshire Parishes in the British Vital Records Index (VRI)
  www.genuki.org.uk/big/eng/STS/VRI.html

- IGI Batch Numbers: Staffordshire Batch Numbers
  freepages.genealogy.rootsweb.com/~tyeroots/staff.html

- IGI Batch Numbers for Stafford, England
  freepages.genealogy.rootsweb.com/~hughwallis/IGIBatchNumbers/
  CountyStafford_(A-M).htm
  Continued at **/CountyStafford_(N-Z).htm**

Transcript Collections on the Web
- Church of England Parish Registers
  www.wolverhamptonarchives.dial.pipex.com/par-registers.htm
  Collection of online indexes on the Wolverhampton Archives site. Individual pages listed below separately

- Transcripts of Nonconformist Registers
  www.wolverhamptonarchives.dial.pipex.com/noncon-regs.htm
  Collection of transcripts on the Wolverhampton Archives site, separately listed here.

Publications
- B.M.S.G.H. Bookshop: Staffordshire: Parishes, Census Districts & Other Places
  www.bmsgh.org/bookshop/staffs/st_a.html
  Lists parish registers and monumental inscriptions available in fiche and book formats

- Staffordshire Parish Register Society
  www.staffs-prs.freeserve.co.uk/

Lookups
- Staffordshire Lookup Exchange
  freespace.virgin.net/m/harbach/sts.html
  Offers lookups of many parish registers and monumental inscriptions

Aldridge
- Aldridge Churches
  www.walsall.gov.uk/localhistorycentre/aldchurch.asp
  List of registers at Walsall Local History Centre

Betley
- Betley Parish Registers 1538-1812
  www.jcorness.fsnet.co.uk/parish%20registers/Registers%20frame.htm
  From the edition published in 1916

Bilston
- Bilston: St. Leonard's Church Registers: Registers of Baptisms 1686-1812, Marriages 1686-1754 and Burials 1727-1812
  www.wolverhamptonarchives.dial.pipex.com/stleonard.htm
  Surname index

- Swan Bank Wesleyan Methodist Church: Transcripts of Church Registers
  www.wolverhamptonarchives.dial.pipex.com/pdf.files/non-con/
  swanbank-baps.pdf
  Index to Bilston baptisms, 1816-1838

- Bilston: Swan Bank Methodist: Burials 1823-1837
  www.wolverhamptonarchives.dial.pipex.com/swanb-bur.htm
  Index

Blackheath
- St. Paul's, Blackheath Baptisms, Marriages and Burials
  uk-transcriptions.accessgenealogy.com/St.Paul's,Blackheath.htm
  Covers 1870-1929

Blakenhall
- Blakenhall Churches
  www.walsall.gov.uk/localhistorycentre/blakchurch.asp
  List of registers at Walsall Local History Centre

Bloxwich
- Bloxwich Churches
  www.walsall.gov.uk/localhistorycentre/bloxchurch.asp
  List of registers at Walsall Local History Centre

Brownhills

See Ogley Hay

Cradley Heath

- St. Luke's, Cradley Heath Baptisms, Marriages & Burials
  **uk-transcriptions.accessgenealogy.com/
  St.Luke's,Cradley%20Heath.htm**
  Covers 1849-1967

Darlaston

- Darlaston Churches
  www.walsall.gov.uk/localhistorycentre/darlchurch.asp
  List of registers at Walsall Local History Centre

Great Barr

- Great Barr Churches
  www.walsall.gov.uk/localhistorycentre/gtbarchurch.asp
  List of registers at Walsall Local History Centre

Kingswinford

- St. Mary's, Kingswinford Marriages & Baptisms (Partial Transcription)
  uk-transcriptions.accessgenealogy.com/St.Mary's,Kingswinford.htm
  Covers 1838-1864

Knutton

- Knutton, Staffordshire, Baptisms, Burials & Marriages
  uk-transcriptions.accessgenealogy.com/Knutton.htm
  20th c.

Longton

- SS. Mary & Chad Marriages (1899-1937)
  geocities.com/bjmargetson/MaryChadMarriages.htm
  At Longton

Moxley

- Moxley Churches
  www.walsall.gov.uk/localhistorycentre/moxchurch.asp
  List of registers at Walsall Local History Centre

Newcastle under Lyme

- St. Gile's, Newcastle Births & Marriages (Various)
  uk-transcriptions.accessgenealogy.com/St.Gile's.htm
  1777-1811. Incomplete?

Ogley Hay

- Ogley Hay/Brownhills Churches
  www.walsall.gov.uk/localhistorycentre/brownchurch.asp
  List of registers at Walsall Local History Centre

Old Hill

- Holy Trinity, Old Hill Baptisms & Marriages
  uk-transcriptions.accessgenealogy.com/Holy%20Trinity.htm
  Covers 1876-1908. Continued to 1920 at
  /Holy%20Trinity%20Baptisms.htm

- Tabernacle, Old Hill Baptisms & Marriages (Partial)
  uk-transcriptions.accessgenealogy.com/Tabernacle,Old%20Hill.htm
  Covers 1909-1958

Pelsall

- Pelsall Churches
  www.walsall.gov.uk/localhistorycentre/pelchurch.asp
  List of registers at Walsall Local History Centre

Rowley Regis

- St. Gile's, Rowley Regis Baptisms, Marriages & Burials
  uk-transcriptions.accessgenealogy.com/St.Giles,Rowley%20Regis.htm
  18-19th c.

- Extracts from the Burial Register of Rowley Regis, Staffordshire
  privatewww.essex.ac.uk/~alan/articles/Rowley.html
  Brief extracts, 1794-1812

Rushall

- Rushall Churches
  www.walsall.gov.uk/localhistorycentre/ruschurch.asp
  List of registers at Walsall Local History Centre

Sedgley

- Extracts from the Sedgley Parish Registers
  members.iinet.net.au/~inphase/sedgley/registers__front.html
  Covers 1558-63

Short Heath

- Short Heath Churches
  www.walsall.gov.uk/localhistorycentre/shortchurch.asp
  List of registers at Walsall Local History Centre

Silverdale
- St. Luke's, Silverdale, Staffordshire Births, Burials & Marriages
  uk-transcriptions.accessgenealogy.com/Silverdale.htm
  Covers 1879-1991

Swynnerton
- St. Mary's Church, Swynnerton: Church Records
  www.btinternet.com/~st.marys/
  Click on 'features' and 'church records'. Covers 1558-1711.

Walsall
- Walsall Churches
  www.walsall.gov.uk/localhistorycentre/walchurch.asp
  List of registers at Walsall Local History Centre

Walsall Wood
- Walsall Wood Churches
  www.walsall.gov.uk/localhistorycentre/walwdchurch.asp
  List of registers at Walsall Local History Centre

Wednesbury
- Wednesbury, St. John: Burials
  www.genuki.org.uk/big/eng/STS/Wednesbury/StJohn/BurialsAC.html
  Index. Continued on 3 further pages

Wednesfield
- Wednesfield: St. Thomas's Church Registers: Registers of Baptisms 1751-1837 and burials 1751-1837
  www.wolverhamptonarchives.dial.pipex.com/stthomas__index1.htm
  Surname index

West Bromwich
- All Saints West Bromwich: Marriages 1821
  familyties6.homestead.com/ASWB17.html
  Continued to 1837 on 16 further pages. For index, see
  www.geocities.com/ann__margetson/allsaintswb.htm

Willenhall
- Willenhall Churches
  www.walsall.gov.uk/localhistorycentre/willenchurch.asp
  List of registers at Walsall Local History Centre

- Willenhall: St. Giles' Church Registers: Registers of Baptisms 1642-1812 and Burials 1727-1812
  www.wolverhamptonarchives.dial.pipex.com/stgiles.htm
  Surname index

- Transcript of entries from St. Giles, Willenhall, Parish Registers
  freespace.virgin.net/m.harbach/ah/transcripts.html
  Pages of extracts for 15 different families

Wolverhampton
- Darlington Street Methodist Church: transcripts of Church Registers
  www.wolverhamptonarchives.dial.pipex.com/pdf.files/non-con/
  darlington-st.pdf
  Index, 1793-1837

- Oxford Street Independent Chapel: transcripts of Church Registers
  www.wolverhamptonarchives.dial.pipex.com/pdf/files/non-con/oxf-st.pdf
  Index, 1786-1837

- Wolverhampton: St. Peter's Church Registers: Registers of Baptisms 1539-1812, Marriages 1539-1838, and Burials 1539-1812
  www.wolverhamptonarchives.dial.pipex.com/stpeter__index1.htm
  Surname index

- St. James', Wolverhampton Baptisms & Marriages
  uk-transcriptions.accessgenealogy.com/St.James,Wolverhampton.htm
  Covers 1860-1930

Suffolk

Civil Registration
- Registration Districts of Suffolk in 1836, with Maps and List of Parishes
  www.jhoddy.demon.co.uk/murrels/index.htm

- Registration Districts in Suffolk
  www.fhsc.org.uk/genuki/reg/sfk.htm
  Between 1837 and 1930

Parish & Non-Parochial Registers: Introductory Pages & Lists
- Births, Deaths and Marriages: Parish Records, Church Registers and Bishops' Transcripts, Suffolk
  www.zip.com.au/~rsterry/gen/suffbdm
  List - but no locations

- Suffolk
  www.sog.org.uk/prc/suffolk.html
  Parish registers, printed, typescript, *etc.,* in the library of the Society of Genealogists

- Quaker Family History Society: Suffolk
  www.rootsweb.com/engqfhs/Research/counties/suffolk.htm
  Notes on Quaker records

Indexes
- Parishes covered by Boyd's Marriage Index: Suffolk
  www.englishorigins.com/bmi-parishstats.asp?county=Suffolk

- IGI Batch Numbers: Suffolk Batch Numbers
  freepages.genealogy.rootsweb.com/~tyeroots/suffolk.html

- IGI Batch Numbers for Suffolk, England
  freepages.genealogy.rootsweb.com/~hughwallis/IGIBatchNumbers/
  CountySuffolk.htm

- Batches extracted from Bishop's Transcripts for the whole County of Suffolk
  freepages.genealogy.rootsweb.com/~hughwallis/
  IGISpecialBatches.htm#Suffolk

- A Selection of Military Marriages, Indexed from Newspapers and Books. Mainly covering Suffolk with a few other counties and countries
  homepages.rootsweb.com/~mwi/milmarr.txt

Publications
- Parish Registers available for Purchase in Microform
  www.suffolkcc.gov.uk/sro/parishlist.html
  From Suffolk Record Office

- The Family History Shop
  www.jenlibrary.u-net.com/
  Many transcripts of parish registers and monumental inscriptions for Suffolk, Norfolk and Cornwall for sale

Acton
- The families from Acton, Suffolk
  www.cosford-database.co.uk/acton/index.htm
  Includes information from parish registers

Beccles
- Beccles and Bungay
  www.genuki.org.uk/big/eng/SFK/BecclesandBungay/
  Primarily transcripts of birth marriage and death entries in the *Beccles and Bungay Weekly News,* 1858-69

Brent Eleigh
- The Families of Brent Eleigh
  www.cosford-database.co.uk/beleigh/index.htm
  Includes information from parish registers

Brettenham
- Brettenham, Suffolk
  www.cosford-database.co.uk/brett/index.html
  Includes information from parish registers

Bungay
See also Beccles

Chelsworth
- Chelsworth Families
  www.cosford-database.co.uk/chels/index.html
  Includes information from parish registers

Cockfield
- Cockfield, Suffolk
  www.cosford-database.co.uk/cfield/index.html
  Includes information from parish registers

Cosford Registration District
- The Cosford Database
  www.cosford-database.co.uk
  Details of over 80,000 people mainly from the Cosford and Lavenham Registration Districts, and including births marriages and deaths. Pages for particular parishes are listed separately here

Hadleigh
- Hadleigh, Suffolk
  www.cosford-database.co.uk/hadleigh/index.html
  Includes information from parish registers

Hitcham
- Hitcham Families
  www.cosford-database.co.uk/hitcham/index.html
  Includes information from parish registers

Kettlebaston
- Kettlebaston, Suffolk
  www.cosford-database.co.uk/kettle/index.html
  Includes information from parish registers

Lavenham
- Lavenham, Suffolk
  www.cosford-database.co.uk/lavenham/index.html
  Includes information from parish registers

Lavenham Registration District
  See Cosford Registration District

Lawshall
- Lawshall, Suffolk Families
  www.cosford-database.co.uk/lawshall/index.html
  Includes information from parish registers

Little Saxham
- Little Saxham Parish Registers
  www.little-saxham.suffolk.gov.uk/history/registers.shtml
  In progress

Little Waldingfield
- Little Waldingfield Familys, 1762-1900
  www.cosford-database.co.uk/etw/index.html
  Includes information from parish registers

Long Melford
- Long Melford, Suffolk: details taken from the Long Melford Parish Magazine, October 1882
  homepages.rootsweb.com/~mwi/lmelford.txt
  Includes extracts from parish registers

Lowestoft
- Index of Surnames: Baptisms 1841-53
  www.genuki.org.uk/big/eng/SFK/LowestoftStMargarets/
  LowestoftStMChr.txt

  At St. Margaret's, Lowestoft

- Index of Surnames: Burials 1745-1812
  www.genuki.org.uk/big/eng/SFK/LowestoftSt.Margarets/
  LowestoftStMBu.txt

  At St. Margaret's, Lowestoft

Milden
- Milden Familys
  www.cosford-database.co.uk/milden/index.htm
  Includes information from parish registers

Monks Eleigh
- Monks Eleigh, Suffolk
  www.cosford-database.co.uk/Meleigh/index.html
  Includes information from parish registers

Monks Soham
- Index of Marriages for Monks Soham 1712-1918
  www.genuki.org.uk/big/eng/SFK/MonkSoham/MonkSohamMR.txt

Preston
- Preston St Mary, Suffolk
  www.cosford-database.co.uk/preston/index.html
  Includes information from parish registers

Southwold
- The Southwold Cemetery Index
  www.waveney.gov.uk/cemetery/southwold/southwold.html
  Register index, late 19-20th c.

Stowmarket
- Stowmarket, Suffolk
  www.cosford-database.co.uk/stowmark/index.html
  Includes information from parish registers

Sudbury
- Sudbury St. Peter: Index of Brides and Grooms
  www.genuki.org.uk/big/eng/SFK/SudburyStPeters/SudburyStPMar.txt
  Index to a printed transcript

Thorpe Morieux
- The Families of Thorpe Morieux
  www.cosford-database.co.uk/thorpe/index.html
  Includes information from parish registers

Waveney
- The Royal Naval Patrol Cemetery Index
  www.waveney.gov.uk/cemetery/belleview/belleview.html
  At Waveney (?); register index, late 20th c.

Wickham Skeith
- [Wickham Skeith Baptism Index 1685-1812]
  www.genuki.org.uk/big/eng/SFK/Wickham Skeith/ws__bap2.txt
  Continued to 1900 at **/ws__bap1.txt**

- [Wickham Skeith Marriage Index, 1685-1812]
  www.genuki.org.uk/big/eng/SFK/WickhamSkeith/ws__mar2.txt
  Continued to 1900 at **/ws__mar1.txt**

Woodbridge
- Beaumont Baptist Church Records
  www.btinternet.com/%7Ebeaumontbaptist/Records/index.htm
  At Woodbridge. Births/Baptisms, 1794-1896; marriages 1863-96; deaths
  1793-1837 & 1862-95.

Woolpit
- Transcript of the Parish Register for Woolpit, Suffolk: Index to
  Baptisms Marriages and Burials
  www.btinternet.com/~PBenyon/Den/Woolpit/Index.html
  freepages.genealogy.rootsweb.com/~pbtye/Den/Woolpit/Index.html

Wrentham
- The Wrentham Cemetery Index
  www.waveney.gov.uk/cemetery/wrentham/wrentham.html
  Register index, later 19-20th c.

Warwickshire

Civil Registration
- Registration Districts in Warwickshire
  www.fhsc.org.uk/genuki/reg/war.htm
  Between 1837 and 1930

- Registration Districts for Churches in the Following Areas
  www.genuki.org.uk/big/eng/WAR/birmingham/bregareas.html
  Covers Birmingham, Aston, Kings Norton, Solihull and West Bromwich
  Registration Districts.

Parish & Non-Parochial Registers: Introductory Pages & Lists
- Parish Registers held at Birmingham Central Library
  www.spencer.onlinehome.de/registers.html
  Includes registers, transcripts, fiche, *etc.,* for Staffordshire,
  Warwickshire and Worcestershire. Does not list the substantial
  collections of published registers from other counties.

- Coventry & District Parish Registers: Parish Register Copies held at
  Coventry Archives
  www.covfhs.org/
  Click on 'Research Aids' and 'Church Records'. List.

- Coventry Non-Conformist Registers: Non-Conformist Registers held at
  Coventry Archives
  www.covfhs.org/
  Click on 'Research Aids' and 'Non-conformism'

- Parish Registers
  www.genuki.org.uk/big/eng/WAR/wcl/wclparish.html
  Brief list of registers held by Warwickshire County Library

- Parish Register Copies
  www.shakespeare.org.uk/cms/cms.asp?ID=8
  At Shakespeare Birthplace Trust

- Warwickshire
  www.sog.org.uk/prc/warwickshire.html
  Parish registers, printed, typescript, *etc.,* in the library of the Society
  of Genealogists

- Quaker Family History Society: Warwickshire
  www.rootsweb.com/~engqfhs/Research/counties/warks.htm
  Notes on Quaker records

Indexes
See also Staffordshire
- IGI Batch Numbers for Warwick, England
  **freepages.genealogy.rootsweb.com/~hughwallis/IGIBatchNumbers/
  CountyWarwick__(A-M).htm**
  Continued at **/County Warwick__(N-Z).htm**
- IGI Batch Numbers: Warwickshire Batch Numbers
  freepages.genealogy.rootsweb.com/~tyeroots/warwick.html

Publications
- B.M.S.G.H. Bookshop: Warwickshire
  www.bmsgh.org/bookshop/warw/wa__a.html
  Lists parish registers and monumental inscriptions in fiche and book
  formats
- Coventry Family History Society: Bookshop. Coventry & District
  Parish Registers
  www.covfhs.org/
- Nuneaton and North Warwickshire Family History Society Publications
  www.nnwfhs.org.uk/pubs/shtml
  Includes some registers
- Rugby Family History Group: Microfiche
  www.rugbyfhs.co.uk
  Includes some parish registers
- The Warwickshire Family History Society: Publications
  www.wfhs.org.uk/wfhs5.htm
  Includes some registers *etc.*

Lookups
- [Warwickshire Lookups]
  uk-transcriptions.accessgenealogy.com/Wendy's%20lookups.htm
  Lists registers, *etc.,* that can be looked-up

Birmingham
- Parish Records, Birmingham Library
  www.genuki.org.uk/big/eng/WAR/deloyd/parishrecs.htm
  List of registers for Birmingham held

- Church Registers, Birmingham
www.genuki.org.uk/big/eng/WAR/deloyd/nonconform.htm
List of nonconformist and Roman Catholic registers

- Birmingham BMD 1893
www.genuki.org.uk/big/eng/WAR/deloyd/Various%201893.html

- Index to the Register of St. Martins, Birmingham 1653-1708, part 1
www.genuki.org.uk/big/eng/WAR/deloyd/registerspart1.html

- St. Philips, Birmingham
www.genuki.org.uk/big/eng/WAR/deloyd/stphilipreg.html
Extracts from the marriage register, 1720-37

Foleshill
- [Foleshill]
uk-transcriptions.accessgenealogy.com/Carole%20Eales%20trans.htm
Lists registers available for lookups.

- Marriage Index for Foleshill, Warwickshire
www.hunimex.com/warwick/foleshill__marriages__g.html

- Foleshill St. Laurence Burials
www.genuki.org.uk/big/eng/WAR/deloyd/Foleshillburials.html
Surname index to 1843

Stretton on Fosse
- Parish Register Transcripts, Stretton-on-Fosse, County of Warwickshire & Diocese of Worcester. Stray Baptisms 1538-1900
members.shaw.ca/panthers2/StrettonBaptismsStrays.html

- Parish Register Transcript, Stretton-on-Fosse: stray marriages 1538-1900
members.shaw.ca/panthers2/StrettonMarriageStrays.html

- Parish Register Transcript, Stretton-on-Fosse, County of Warwickshire & Diocese of Worcester: Stray Burials 1538-1900
members.shaw.ca/panthers2/StrettonBurialStrays.html

- Stretton-on-Fosse, Warwickshire (Parish Registers) Family Charts
www.allthecotswolds.com/
Click on 'sitemap' and title. List of family surnames in the registers

Westmoreland

Civil Registration
See also Northumberland

- Registration Districts in Westmorland
www.fhsc.org.uk/genuki/reg/wes.htm
Between 1837 and 1930

Parish & Non-Parochial Registers: Introductory Pages & Lists
- Westmorland
www.sog.org.uk/prc/westmorland.html
Parish registers, printed, typescript, *etc.,* in the library of the Society of Genealogists

- Quaker Family History Society: Westmorland
www.rootsweb.com/~engqfhs/Research/counties/west.htm
Notes on Quaker records

Indexes
- IGI Batch Numbers: Westmorland Batch Numbers
freepages.genealogy.rootsweb.com/~tyeroots/westmor.html

- IGI Batch Numbers for Westmorland, England
freepages.genealogy.rootsweb.com/~hughwallis/IGIBatchNumbers/CountyWestmorland.htm

Askham
- Askham Parish Registers
edenlinks.rootsweb.com/1gp/RECORDS/ASKIND.HTM
Covers 1566-1670, plus marriages and banns 1754-1812

Beetham
- Beetham Parish Registers
edenlinks.rootsweb.com/beetham/INDEX__PAGE.HTM
Covers 1690-1749

Cliburn
- Cumbrian Genealogy: Cliburn Parish Register 1565-1812
johnwatters.members.beeb.net/CliburnAtoL.htm
Continued at **/CliburnMtoz.htm**

Crosby Ravensworth
- Cumbrian Genealogy: Crosby Ravensworth; Births, Marriages & Deaths 1570-1812
  johnwatters.members.beeb.net/CrosRavA.htm
  Continued on 13 further pages

Kendal
- Cumbrian Genealogy: the Registers of Kendal
  johnwatters.beeb.net/Ken1558a.htm
  Covers 1558-87. Index, continued on 2 further pages.

- Cumbrian Genealogy: Kendal Baptisms 1596-99, Marriages and Burials 1591-99 and Baptisms 1607-31
  johnwatters.beeb.net/Kendal3A.htm
  Continued on 14 further pages

Kirkby Thore
- Cumbrian Genealogy: Kirkby Thore Registers: Miscellaneous Entries
  johnwatters.beeb.net/Kythore.html
  Parish register extracts, 1652-1724, originally published in the *Cumberland and Westmorland Antiquarian and Archaeological Society transactions,* 1879

Milburn
- Cumbrian Genealogy: Milburn Parish Register 1679-1812
  johnwatters.beeb.net/MilburnAtoG.htm
  Index, continued on 2 further pages

Yorkshire

Civil Registration
- Registration Districts in Yorkshire; East Riding
  www.fhsc.org.uk/genuki/reg/ery.htm
  Between 1837 and 1930

- Registration Districts in Yorkshire; North Riding
  www.fhsc.org.uk/genuki/reg/nry.htm
  Between 1837 and 1930

- Registration Districts in Yorkshire; West Riding
  www.fhsc.org.uk/genuki/reg/wry.htm
  Between 1837 and 1930

- [St. Catherine's House Marriage Index, Jan-March, 1849. District 22. Yorkshire]
  www.cs.ncl.ac.uk/genuki/StCathsTranscriptions/CATH4922.TXT

- [St. Catherine's House Marriage Index, Jan-March, 1849. District 23. Yorkshire]
  www.cs.ncl.ac.uk/genuki/StCathsTranscriptions/CATH4923.TXT

- Middlesbrough Indexes
  www.ndfhs.org.uk/RegIndex.html
  Index to registers held at Middlesbrough, Stockton-on-Tees, Redcar and Cleveland Register Offices

- Sheffield & District Family History Society: Registration Districts
  www.sheffieldfhs.org.uk/serv_con/reg.htm
  List of parishes and their registration districts in Sheffield area

- Yorkshire BMD: Births Marriages and Deaths on the Internet
  www.yorkshirebmd.org.uk/
  Project to index civil registration records since 1837

Parish & Non-Parochial Registers: Introductory Pages & Lists
- Parish Records at the Borthwick Institute
  www.york.ac.uk/inst/bihr/prs.htm
  List of original registers held

- Papers Relating to Parish Registers
  www.york.ac.uk/inst/bihr/guideprt.pdf
  At the Borthwick Institute

- Records of Peculiar Jurisdictions
  www.york.ac.uk/inst/bihr/guidepec.pdf
  Including bishops transcripts, marriage bonds *etc.*

- Parish Registers
  www.doncaster.gov.uk/education/document.asp?WSDOCID=1229
  List of those held by Doncaster Archives

- Non-Parochial Registers
  www.doncaster.gov.uk/education/document.asp?WSOCID=1225
  List of registers on fiche held by Doncaster Archives

- Bishop's Transcripts
  www.doncaster.gov.uk/education/document.asp?WSDOCID=1197
  List of microfilm held by Doncaster Archives

- Cemeteries
  www.doncaster.gov.uk/education/document.asp?WSDOCID1205
  List of cemetery registers held by Doncaster Archives (originals and microfilm)

- Handlist of Parish Registers on Deposit
  www.eastriding.gov.uk/learning/archives/pdf/prnet.pdf
  At East Riding Archives

- Handlist of Non-Anglican Church Records
  www.eastriding.gov.uk/learning/archives/pdf/ncnet.pdf
  At East Riding Archives

- Handlist of Society of Friends and Non-Paorhcial Registers on Microfilm
  www.eastriding.gov.uk/learning/archives/pdf/mfnet.pdf

- Cemetery Records
  www.eastriding.gov.uk/learning/archives/pdf/cemnet.pdf
  At East Riding Archives

- Archival Collections: Parish Records: A List
  www.hull.ac.uk/lib/archives/parish.html
  At the University of Hull; includes a few transcripts of registers

- Yorkshire
  www.sog.org.uk/prc/yks.html
  Parish registers, printed, typescript, *etc.,* in the library of the Society of Genealogists

- Yorkshire Parish Registers in the Australian National Library
  www.pcug.org.au/~bthompso/natlib/yprxy.txt
  List of published registers

- Quaker Family History Society: Yorkshire
  www.rootsweb.com/~engqfhs/Research/counties/yorks.htm
  Notes on Quaker records

Marriage Licences

- Yorkshire: Paver's Marriage Licences for the Year 1567 to 1628
  www.genuki.org.uk/big/eng/YKS/Misc/Transcriptions/YKS/PaversIndex.html
  From the *Yorkshire Archaeological and Topographical Journal*

- Marriage Bonds
  www.york.ac.uk/inst/bihr/marbnds.htm
  General discussion of bonds for York Diocese at the Borthwick Institute and elsewhere

Indexes

- Parishes covered by Boyd's Marriage Index: Yorkshire
  www.englishorigins.com/bmi-parishstats.asp?county=Yorkshire

- IGI Batch Numbers: Yorkshire Batch Numbers
  freepages.genealogy.rootsweb.com/~tyeroots/york.html

- IGI Batch Numbers for Yorkshire, England
  freepages.genealogy.rootsweb.com/~hughwallis/IGIBatchNumbers/CountyYorkshire__(A-D).HTM

  Continued on 5 further pages

- The Pontefract & District Family History Society Search Services
  freespace.virgin.net/richard.lockwood/
  Details of parish register and monumental inscription databases, *etc.*

Publications

- Cemetery Burial Registers
  www.doncasterfhs.freeserve.co.uk
  Click on 'Publications' and title

- Burial Index
  www.doncasterfhs.freeserve.co.uk
  Click on 'Publications' and title. Indexes available from Doncaster Family History Society

- Huddersfield & District Family History Society Publications
  www.hdfhs.org.uk/fhspubtp.htm
  Includes parish registers

- The Pontefract and District Family History Society: Publications
  freespace.virgin.net/richard.lockwood/
  Includes baptism, marriage and burial indexes, *etc.*

- Rotherham Family History Society Publications
  www.rotherhamfhs.f9.co.uk
  Includes a few registers

- Sheffield & District Family History Society: Society Publications: Microfiche
  www.sheffieldfhs.org.uk/Pub__con/micro-fiche.htm
  Includes register transcripts and indexes

- Sheffield & District Family History Society: Society Publications: 3.5 inch Computer Disks
  www.sheffieldfhs.org.uk/Pub__con/comp-disk.htm
  Includes burial indexes

- Wakefield & District Family History Society: Society Publications
  www.wdfhs.co.uk/publications.html
  Includes marriage and burial indexes, parish registers, monumental inscriptions, *etc.*

- Wharfedale Family History Group Publications
  www.users.globalnet.co.uk/~gdl/wfhg3.htm
  Includes parish and nonconformist registers, memorial inscriptions, *etc.*

- The City of York & District Family History Society: Society Publications
  www.yorkfamilyhistory.org.uk/books.htm
  Includes parish registers and indexes, *etc.*

- Brian Jones
  www.brianjoneswry.co.uk
  Includes various transcripts of West Riding parish registers for sale

Ackworth

- Ackworth St. Cuthbert, Yorkshire: Parish Register Transcriptions
  freepages.genealogy.rootsweb.com/~petyt/ackprt.htm
  Baptisms 1813-40; banns 1823-53

Batley Carr

- Batley Carr: Transcription of the Baptisms 1841-1862
  www.genuki.org.uk/big/eng/YKS/Misc/Transcriptions/WRY/
  BatleyCarrBaptisms.html
  Continued to 1866 at **/BatleyCarrBaptisms1863__1866.html**

Bolsterstone

- Bolsterstone Genealogy Project
  www.bolsterstone.de/Church%20Registers.htm
  Index to baptisms, 1778-1872

- Bolsterstone Genealogy Project
  www.bolsterstone.de/Marriages.htm
  Marriages 1868-1905

- Bolsterstone: Transcription of Bolsterstone Marriages
  www.genuki.org.uk/big/eng/YKS/Misc/Transcriptions/WRY/
  BolsterstoneMarriages1868-77.html

Bradford

- Name Index to Bradford Church Burials 1681-1837
  www.genuki.org.uk/big/eng/YKS/bfhs/pcbur81.html
  Details of published indexes for sale

Brawby

See Salton

Burghwallis

- Burghwallis Roman Catholic Church Baptisms
  www.doncasterfhs.freeserve.co.uk/members/
  Click on title. Downloadable files for 1761-1782 and 1798-1836, for members of Doncaster Family History Society only

Burmantofts

- Beckett Street Cemetery
  www.fobsc.20m.com/
  Also known as Burmantofts Cemetery, Leeds. Introduction; includes fiche for sale of the burial and grave registers and inscriptions

Calverley

- Calverley Parish Baptisms Index 1574-1644
  www.genuki.org.uk/big/eng/YKS/Misc/Transcriptions/WRY/
  CalverleyBaptismsIndex1574-1644.html

- Calverley: Calverley Parish Registers: Baptisms
  www.genuki.org.uk/big/eng/YKS/Misc/Transcriptions/WRY/
  CalverleyBaptisms1574-1597.html
  Covers 1574-96. Continued to 1644 on 3 further pages

- Calverley: All legible Baptisms and Births recorded at the Parish Church of Calverley for Families in the Idle / Thackley / Windhill area 1726 to 1745
  www.genuki.org.uk/big/eng/YKS/Misc/Transcriptions/WRY/
  Calverley__IdleBaptisms1726-45.html

- Calverley Parish Marriage Index 1596-1720
  www.genuki.org.uk/big/eng/YKS/Misc/Transcriptions/WRY/
  CalverleyMarriagesIndex1596-1720.html

- Parish Church of Calverley: Marriages 1813 to 1834: sorted alphabetically by Groom
  www.genuki.org.uk/big/eng/YKS/MISC/Transcriptions/WRY/
  CalverleyMarriagesGrooms1813-34.html
  For brides, see **/CalverleyMarriages1813-34.html**

- Calverley Parish Burials
  www.calverley.info/cal__bur.htm
  Covers 1596-1720

- Calverley Parish Burials Index 1596-1720
  www.genuki.org.uk/big/eng/YKS/Misc/Transcriptions/WRY/
  CalverleyBurialsIndex1596-1720.html

  See also Idle

Cayton

- Cayton: Transcription of Baptisms from the Film of the Bishops' Transcripts
  www.genuki.org.uk/big/eng/YKS/Misc/Transcriptions/NRY/
  CaytonBaptisms1812to1860.html
  Covers 1812-37 and 1860

- Cayton: Transcription of Marriages from the Film of the Bishop's Transcripts
  www.genuki.org.uk/big/eng/YKS/Misc/NRY/
  CaytonMarriages1812to1860.html
  Covers 1812-37

- Cayton: Transcription of Burials from the Film of the Bishop's Transcripts
  www.genuki.org.uk/big/eng/YKS/Misc/Transcriptions/NRY/
  CaytonBurials1812to1860.html

Dewsbury

- Dewsbury: Transcription of the Dewsbury Baptisms 1841 to 1866
  www.genuki.org.uk/big/eng/YKS/Misc/Transcriptions/WRY/
  DewsburyBaptisms1841-66.html

- Dewsbury Transcription of the Burials 1813 to 1817
  www.genuki.org.uk/big/eng/YKS/Misc/Transcriptions/WRY/
  DewsburyBurials1813to1817.html
  Continued to 1822 at **/DewsburyBurials1818to1822.html**

- Dewsbury: Transcription of the Dewsbury Burials, Jan 1885 to Feb 1886
  www.genuki.org.uk/big/eng/YKS/Misc/Transcriptions/WRY/
  DewsburyBurials1855-86.html

Doncaster

- St. George's Burials 1578-1855
  www.doncasterfhs.freeserve.co.uk/members/
  Click on title. Downloadable file for Doncaster Family History Society members only

Eccleshill

- Norman Lane Burial Ground, Eccleshill, Bradford (1823-1984)
  www.genuki.org.uk/big/eng/YKS/bfhs/nlbg.html
  Details of published registers *etc.,* for sale

Elland

- Elland Parish Church: Marriages 1754 to 1812
  www.whitwam.freeserve.co.uk/ell.htm
  Details of indexes for sale

Forcett

- Forcett: Transcription of the Baptisms 1596 to 1649
  www.genuki.org.uk/big/eng/YKS/Misc/Transcriptions/NRY/
  ForcettBaptisms1596__1707.html

- Forcett: Transcription of the Baptisms 1813 to 1857
  www.genuki.org.uk/big/eng/YKS/Misc/Transcriptions/NRY/
  ForcettBaptisms1813__1857.html
  Continued to 1861 at **/Forcett Baptisms1857__1861.html**

- Forcett: Transcription of the Burials 1813-1898
  www.genuki.org.uk/big/eng/YKS/Misc/Transcriptions/NRY/
  ForcettBurials1813__1898.html

- Forcett: Transcription of the Forcett Marriages 1606-1812
  www.genuki.org.uk/big/eng/YKS/Misc/Transcriptions/NRY/
  ForcettMarriages1597__1812.html

Halifax

- Halifax Parish Church Registers 1542-5
  www.genuki.org.uk/big/eng/YKS/WRY/Halifax/Halifax1542.html
  Transcribed from *Yorkshire County Magazine*

Hartshead

- Hartshead: Transcription of the St. Peter's, Hartshead Burials, 1692 to 1722
  www.genuki.org.uk/big/eng/YKS/Misc/Transcriptions/WRY/
  HartsheadStPeterBur1692-1733.html
  Continued to 1812 on 2 further pages

- Hartshead Burials 1890-93
  freepages.genealogy.rootsweb.com/~hartsheadcumclifton/
  hartshead/bur.htm

Hatfield

- Hatfield Parish Register Extracts
  freepages.genealogy.rootsweb.com/~maureenbryson/id52.htm
  Selected surnames only

High Bentham

- Low Bentham parish: High Bentham Burials Transcription
  www.genuki.org.uk/big/eng/YKS/WRY/Lowbentham/
  BrHighBenthamBurials.html

  Covers 1944-2000

Horbury

- Horbury: Transcription of Horbury Baptisms and Burials 1770 to 1791
  www.genuki.org.uk/big/eng/YKS/Misc/Transcriptions/WRY/
  HorburyBapBur1770-1791.html
  Continued to 1812 on 3 further pages

- Horbury Marriages 1774 to 1812
  www.genuki.org.uk/big/eng/YKS/Misc/Transcriptions/WRY/
  HorburyMar1774-1812.html

Huddersfield

- Huddersfield Parish Church Marriages 1754 to 1837
  www.whitwam.freeserve.co.uk/hpcm2.htm
  Details of indexes for sale

Idle

- Calverley Parish Registers, Idle Chapel Baptisms 1796 to 1800
  www.genuki.org.uk/big/eng/YKS/Misc/Transcriptions/WRY/
  IdleChapelBaptisms1796-1800.html

Kilnwick on the Wolds

- All Saints Church Parish Registers, Kilnwick on the Wolds, ERY
  members.netscape.online.co.uk/pbtyc/Den/Kilnwick/Index.html
  Early 19th c.

- Kilnwick on the Wolds: Transcript from All Saints Parish Register, Kilnwick on the Wolds ERY: Baptisms 1813-1828
  www.genuki.org.uk/big/eng/YKS/Misc/Transcriptions/ERY/
  KilnwickBaptisms1813-1828.html
  Continued to 1841 at **/KilnwickBaptisms1829-1841.html**
  Indexed at **/KilnwickBaptismsChildIndex1813-1841.html**

- Kilnwick on the Wolds: Transcription of the Kilnwick on the Wolds Parish Register: Banns 1823-1841

  www.genuki.org.uk/big/eng/YKS/Misc/Transcriptions/ERY/
  KilnwickBanns1823-1841.html
  Indexed at /KilnwickBannsIndex1823-41.html
- Kilnwick on the Wolds: Transcript from All Saints Parish Register, Kilnwick on the Wolds, ERY: Marriages 1813-1841
  www.genuki.org.uk/big/eng/YKS/Misc/Transcriptions/ERY/
  KilnwickMarriages1813-1841.html
  Indexed at /KilnwickMarriagesIndex1813-1841.html
- Kilnwick on the Wolds: Transcript from All Saints Parish Register, Kilnwick on the Wolds ERY: Burials 1813-1841
  www.genuki.org.uk/big/eng/YKS/Misc/Transcriptions/ERY/
  KilnwickBurials1813-1841.html
  Indexed at /KilnwickBurialsIndex1813-1841.html

Leeds
- Records of Churches / Places of Worship (Parish Records)
  leedsindexers.co.uk/Parish.htm
  List for Leeds
- Leeds Parish Registers 1612-1639
  www.bigenealogy.com/leeds/
  As published by the Thoresby Society

Malton
- Transcriptions of the Births Marriages and Deaths from the *Malton Messenger* for the year 1854
  www.genuki.org.uk/big/eng/YKS/Misc/Transcriptions/NRY/
  MaltonMessenger1854BDM.html
  Further annual pages cover the period to 1861
- Births Marriages & Deaths from the *Malton Messenger* 1854
  www.angelfire.com/de/BobSanders/Malton54.html
  Continued to 1860 on 10 further pages

Normanby
- Transcript of St. Andrews Parish Church, Normanby, NRY, Parish Registers
  freepages.genealogy.rootsweb.com/~pbtyc/Den/Normanby/index.html
  Baptisms 1699-1812; marriages 1699-1837; burials 1700-1812

- Normanby: Transcription of the Parish Registers: Baptisms 1699-1774
  www.genuki.org.uk/big/eng/YKS/Misc/Transcriptions/NRY/
  NormanbyBaptisms1699.html
  Continued to 1812 at /NormanbyBaptisms1775.html
  Indexed at /NormanbyBaptismsIndex.html
- Normanby: Transcription of the Normanby Parish Registers: Marriages 1699-1750
  www.genuki.org.uk/big/eng/YKS/Misc/Transcriptions/NRY/
  NormanbyMarriages1699-1750.html
  Continued to 1837 (including index) on 3 further pages
- Normanby: Transcription of the Normanby Parish Registers: Burials 1700-1812
  www.genuki.org.uk/big/eng/YKS/Misc/Transcriptions/NRY/
  NormanbyBurials1700-1812.html
  Indexed at /NormanbyBurialsIndex.html
- Normanby Parish Registers: Burials: Notes
  www.genuki.org.uk/big/eng/YKS/Misc/Transcriptions/NRY/
  NormanbyPRNotes.html

Northowram
- Nonconformist Register of Baptisms, Marriages and Deaths ... 1644-1702, 1702-1752, generally known as the Northowram or Coley Register, but comprehending numerous notices of puritans and anti-puritans in Yorkshire, Lancashire, Cheshire, London, &c.
  www.genuki.org.uk/big/eng/YKS/northowram/
  From a printed book published 1881

Rawmarsh
See Wath upon Dearne

Roos
- Roos Parish Registers
  www.pcug.org.au/~bthompso/roos/roos.htm
  Scanned transcript of a register originally published 1888, covering 1571-1679.

Rosedale
- Rosedale People: an index
  www.genuki.org.uk/big/eng/YKS/Misc/Transcriptions/
  NRYRosedale/index.html
  Sources indexed include parish registers and monumental inscriptions

Rotherham

- Rotherham Parish Register Extracts
  freepages.genealogy.rootsweb.com/~maureenbryson/id51.htm
  Selected surnames only

Salton

- Index to Transcription from St. John's Parish Register, Salton and Brawby, Vale of Pickering, NRY, for the period 1573-1837
  freepages.genealogy.rootsweb.com/~pbtyc/Den/
  Salton__and__Brawby/Index.html

- Salton: Transcript from St. John's Parish Register, Salton and Brawby, Vale of Pickering, NRY: Baptisms 1573-1600
  www.genuki.org.uk/big/eng/YKS/Misc/Transcriptions/NRY/
  SaltonBaptisms1573-1600.html
  Continued to 1837 on 5 further pages

- Salton: Transcript from St. John's Parish Register, Salton and Brawby, Vale of Pickering, NRY: Child Baptism Index
  www.genuki.org.uk/big/eng/YKS/Misc/Transcriptions/NRY/
  SaltonBaptismsChildIndex.html

- Salton: Transcript from St. John's Parish Register, Salton and Brawby, Vale of Pickering, NRY: Father Baptisms Index
  www.genuki.org.uk/big/eng/YKS/Misc/Transcriptions/NRY/
  SaltonBaptismsFatherIndex.html

- Salton: Transcript from St. John's Parish Register, Salton and Brawby, Vale of Pickering, NRY: Mother Baptisms Index
  www.genuki.org.uk/big/eng/YKS/Misc/Transcriptions/NRY/
  SaltonBaptismsMotherIndex.html

- Salton: Transcript from St. John's Parish Register, Salton and Brawby, Vale of Pickering, NRY: Marriages 1573-1650
  www.genuki.org.uk/big/eng/YKS/Misc/Transcriptions/NRY/
  SaltonMarriages1573-1650.html
  Continued to 1837 on 5 further pages

- Salton: Transcript from St. John's Parish Register, Salton and Brawby, Vale of Pickering, NRY. Marriages: Brides Index 1574-1736
  www.genuki.org.uk/big/eng/YKS/Misc/Transcriptions/NRY/
  SaltonMarriagesBridesIndex1574-1736.html
  See also Grooms index at
  /SaltonMarriagesGroomsIndex1574-1736.html

- Salton: Transcript from St. John's Parish Register, Salton and Brawby, Vale of Pickering; NRY: Marriages, Bride and Groom Index
  www.genuki.org.uk/big/eng/YKS/Misc/Transcriptions/NRY/
  SaltonMarriagesBGIndex1737-1837.html

- Salton: Transcript from St. John's Parish Register, Salton and Brawby, Vale of Pickering, NRY: Marriages Witness 1 Index
  www.genuki.org.uk/big/eng/YKS/Misc/Transcriptions/NRY/
  SaltonMarriagesWitness1Index1737-1837.html
  Continued at **/SaltonMarriagesWitness2Index1737-1837.html**

Sandtoft

- Sandtoft
  privatewww.essex.ac.uk/%7Ealan/family/G-Sandtoft.html
  Extracts from a Huguenot register, 17th c.

Sheffield

- Sheffield & District BDM Registers: Timelines
  sheffieldfhs.org.uk/data/registers.html
  List of registers and dates

- Sheffield & District Family History Society: Transcription Projects
  www.sheffieldfhs.org.uk/serv__con/transcrips.html
  Details of the society's Burials transcriptions project, *etc.*

South Milford

- South Milford: Transcription of the Burials 1847 to 1979
  www.genuki.org.uk/big/eng/YKS/Misc/transcriptions/WRY/
  SouthMilfordBurials1847__1979.html
  Continued to 1998 at **/SouthMilfordBurials1979__1998.html**

Staincross

- Burial Register for St. John the Evangelist Church, Staincross
  freepages.genealogy.rootsweb.com/~framland/stcr/stjscd1.htm
  Index, continued on 9 further pages

Thorne

- Thorne Parish Register Extracts
  freepages.genealogy.rootsweb.com/≈maureenbryson/id53.htm
  Selected surnames only

Thornton Bell

- Thornton Bell Chapel Registers
  www.genuki.org.uk/big/eng/YKS/bfhs/thrntnbc.html
  Details of published indexes for sale

Wakefield
- Burials in the Parish Church
  freepages.genealogy.rootsweb.com/~framland/CHURCH/burials.htm
  At Wakefield

Wath upon Dearne
- Wath & Dearne Valley Resources Site
  www.gleaden.plus.com/index.htm
  Click on 'parish registers'. Includes Wath baptisms 1598-1778; marriages 1598-1779; burials 1598-1778; also for Rawmarsh, baptisms 1653-1672; marriages 1575-1753; burials 1558-1633

Whitkirk
- Whitkirk: Transcription of the Burials 1875-1879
  **www.genuki.org.uk/big/eng/YKS/Misc/Transcriptions/WRY/
  WhitkirkBurials1875to9.html**

Worsbrough
- Swaithe Main Colliery Disaster, Worsbrough
  www.barnsleyfhs.co.uk/swaithe1.htm
  List of miners killed, 1875